What people are saying about

Friday's Child

Brian Mountford's engagement with religion, and with the world, and with the human aspects of them both, has been something I've long admired. In this inspiring collection of poems and readings for Good Friday he brings all his experience of literature, and of the needs of readers and listeners both young and old, together to create a tapestry of great brilliance and a commentary of calm wisdom.
Philip Pullman

Brian Mountford has written a short reflection on each poem in this wonderful collection – insightful, often understated and spacious so as to encourage our own response. What a clever idea and so beautifully done. This is an anthology that will feed the soul throughout the year.
Nicholas Holtam, Bishop of Salisbury

Teenagers who originally read these poems in public on Good Friday

It was interesting having poems that you wouldn't normally associate with Good Friday; yet including them made you reflect on them in a different way. It's good not to compartmentalise religion or to say only 'religious' things can be spiritual. (Jerome Gasson)

Reading these poems on Good Friday was always an important part of my year. They opened up discussions about doubt, religious doctrine, and human nature for me. This is how young people want to be treated; we never felt patronised, but our voices were, in every sense, heard. (Aphra Hiscock)

Saying poetry aloud and thinking how you are going to make it sound (or how others might hear it) makes you think much more about what it might be trying to say. (Julius Gasson)

Being part of the group gave a chance for us to offer something to a wider community. We liked the way visitors chancing by might stop and be moved to listen. (All)

Friday's Child

Poems of Suffering and Redemption

Friday's Child

Poems of Suffering and Redemption

Brian Mountford

CHRISTIAN
ALTERNATIVE

Winchester, UK
Washington, USA

First published by Christian Alternative Books, 2018
Christian Alternative Books is an imprint of John Hunt Publishing Ltd.,
No. 3 East St., Alresford, Hampshire SO24 9EE, UK
office1@jhpbooks.net
www.johnhuntpublishing.com
www.christian-alternative.com

For distributor details and how to order please visit the 'Ordering' section on our website.

Text copyright: Brian Mountford 2017

ISBN: 978 1 78535 741 1
978 1 78535 742 8 (ebook)
Library of Congress Control Number: 2017944842

A CIP catalogue record for this book is available from the British Library.

Design: Stuart Davies

Printed and bound by CPI Group (UK) Ltd, Croydon, CR0 4YY, UK

We operate a distinctive and ethical publishing philosophy in all areas of our business, from our global network of authors to production and worldwide distribution.

Contents

Introduction

For thirty years I was the vicar of 'the most visited parish church' in England, The University Church of St Mary the Virgin, Oxford. During the Easter holidays we were always overwhelmed by tourists and, if it was sunny, the churchyard would be full of the clatter of coffee cups and chatter. But on Good Friday we used to close the church, only allowing in the devout few who wished to attend the Three Hour Service. This was intended as a mark of respect, witnessing to 'the world', as we thought, the solemnity of this sacred day when Christian values of self-giving and unconditional love challenged the shallowness of consumerism.

Then I noticed how many people, especially from catholic countries, were puzzled and angry, unable to understand why they were excluded. What began as a good intention ended up sending out entirely the wrong message. So I decided to open the church all day and to put on a programme of events where people could drop in for as little or as much time as they liked. I wanted to show that sacred and secular could exist side by side and hoped something of the Easter message might rub off. We enacted the Stations of the Cross (scenes from the Passion of Christ) in a procession that went into the surrounding streets; the choir gave a concert of Passiontide music; and for half an hour teenage members of the congregation read poems and prose passages related to the Passion, which they did with great intelligence and dignity. Thus, for the past eight years, I have been selecting readings for Good Friday, which are collected here, each one with a short commentary attached. I have not augmented the collection in any kind of attempt to provide a fully representative anthology, but kept it exactly as it evolved in response to this specific need to share a little seriousness with the holiday crowd.

Some poems, like John Skelton's 'Woefully Arrayed' or John Donne's 'Good Friday, 1613, Riding Westward', choose themselves; others, like Philip Larkin's 'Ambulances', Seamus Heaney's 'Digging' and Wilfred Owen's 'Greater Love', are not immediately obvious. But the Passion of Christ has a universal theme of suffering and redemption that has unfortunately been narrowed by some Christian apologists, determined to privatise it and impose their particular interpretation of its meaning on others. It seemed to me that any serious attempt to write about suffering, betrayal and the search for meaning constitutes a kind of scripture that can amplify what Christians call *Holy Scripture*. For example, I remember once asking why Blake's 'The Tyger' appeared in Helen Gardner's *Faber Book of Religious Verse*. I always pictured it from the eye of a hunter, face-to-face and mesmerised by the 'fearful symmetry'; miss your shot and you're dead meat. What's religious about that? I was slow to catch on that this is about one of the principal objections to Christianity, the problem of evil: why would a loving and all-powerful God allow suffering in the world? Did he who made the lamb also make the tiger?

In this there's a parallel with visual art. The crucifixion is one of the most depicted scenes in classical art, not least because it was the frequent subject of reredos and triptych paintings behind altars in churches all over Europe. Yet the art critic, Neil MacGregor, has argued that the traditional crucifixion scene lost its power as a universal image in the twentieth century because there was too much other suffering. It was replaced by worse images: the slaughter of the trenches, the emaciated prisoners of Auschwitz, and that famous photograph of a Vietnamese girl running down the road burning with napalm. Crucifixion scenes were also transposed by painters from Italian hills into housing estates and amongst city skyscrapers.

None of my teenage readers ever asked why I had chosen a particular piece or complained that a poem wasn't religious enough for Good Friday. They took them in their stride, for what they were, unknowingly sharing Rowan Williams' view that the ideal was not to be a religious poet, but a poet who writes about religious themes. They kept their criticisms to themselves, except when I said that this or that poem couldn't be explained because part of the character of poetry is to provide words that provoke and tease the reader into a thought that might not otherwise occur. I suppose it's the result of reading poetry at school, the idea that literature is susceptible to explanation and unpacking. Why else would you write essays about it? But as Jeannette Winterson says, 'we don't go to Shakespeare to find out about life in Elizabethan England, any more than we read Jane Austen for marriage guidance. Art lasts because it gives us a language for our inner reality... it is a connection across time to all those others who have suffered and failed, found happiness, lost it, faced death, ruin, struggled, survived, known the night-hours of inconsolable pain'. She's not arguing for religion, but surely that is what religion is about too. Religion addresses our most deep experience, our common experience, not some compartmentalised pocket of experience called 'church'. And therefore the insights of agnostic and atheist artists are as important as what one might call 'spiritual' writers, whose confessional approach often leads to a restricted and closed view of life, ethics and the order of things.

Part of what I am trying to achieve now is caught by Marilynne Robinson in her book of essays, *The Givenness of Things*: 'Great theology is always a kind of giant and intricate poetry, like epic or saga. It is written for those who know the tale already, the urgent messages and the dying words, and who attend to its retelling with a special alertness, because the story has a claim on them and they on it. Theology is also close to the spoken voice. It evokes sermon, sacrament, and liturgy, and of course scripture itself, with all its echoes of song and legend and prayer.'

As an addendum to the poems I've included five prayers that we used to punctuate the readings, prayers that were read by ten and eleven-year-old members of the group.

The Tyger by William Blake (1757-1827)

Tyger! Tyger! burning bright
In the forests of the night,
What immortal hand or eye
Could frame thy fearful symmetry?

In what distant deeps or skies
Burnt the fire of thine eyes?
On what wings dare he aspire?
What the hand dare seize the fire?

And what shoulder, & what art,
Could twist the sinews of thy heart?
And when thy heart began to beat,
What dread hand? & what dread feet?

What the hammer? what the chain?
In what furnace was thy brain?
What the anvil? what dread grasp
Dare its deadly terrors clasp?

When the stars threw down their spears,
And watered heaven with their tears,
Did he smile his work to see?
Did he who made the Lamb make thee?

Tyger! Tyger! burning bright
In the forests of the night,
What immortal hand or eye
Dare frame thy fearful symmetry?

Most famous now for his poem, 'And did those feet in ancient time', in its musical setting by Parry sung at cricket matches and weddings, William Blake was a poet, mystic, and painter. 'Tyger, Tyger' is from *Songs of Innocence and Experience* and falls heavily on the experience side of the scales, with 'The Lamb' as its counterbalance on the side of innocence.

'Little Lamb who made thee

Dost thou know who made thee?'

Why would this poem be chosen for Good Friday? Because the creation of a streamlined killing machine tiger symbolises the problem of evil. How can a loving, powerful, creator God allow suffering in the world?

The rhythm of the poem has the clank of a blacksmith's hammer hitting the anvil. But what I like most is that it consists entirely of unanswered questions. This is no sceptical modernist writing, though. It is a visionary Christian poet of 225 years ago.

The fact of these questions is not a declaration of doubt, but a positive readiness to challenge God with an essential paradox of religion (and also of life) that violence and passivity are part of the human condition and part of the physical creation itself. For example, the force of gravity enables life, yet it is a major threat to life. God is in the heat and hazard of the forge as well as in the still small voice of calm.

To question faith is not to deny Christ, but to look for different perspectives. It's like those wonderful moments in Alan Bennett's play *The History Boys* when the maverick teacher, Hector, makes his scholarship class think for themselves, defend their assertions, and see history in a much wider, interdisciplinary context.

It's no accident that William Blake asks whether he who made the Tiger also made the Lamb, and in the text written in Blake's own hand Lamb has a capital letter, referring to the Lamb of God who takes away the sin of the world. Did he who made the rapier thrust also make self-giving love? Did he who made self-giving love also let the soldiers drive nails through his own hands?

How does a loving father look on his son's crucifixion? Answer: it is God himself who suffers. Are you convinced?

Prayer by Carol Ann Duffy (born 1955)

Some days, although we cannot pray, a prayer
utters itself. So a woman will lift
her head from the sieve of her hands and stare
at the minims sung by a tree, a sudden gift.

Some nights, although we are faithless, the truth
enters our hearts, that small familiar pain;
then a man will stand stock-still, hearing his youth
in the distant Latin chanting of a train.

Pray for us now. Grade 1 piano scales
console the lodger looking out across
a Midlands town. Then dusk, and someone calls
a child's name as though they named their loss.

Darkness outside. Inside the radio's prayer -
Rockall. Malin. Dogger. Finisterre.

In this very agnostic take on prayer, Carol Ann Duffy is clearly not writing about Good Friday. So why include it here? Because, indirectly, I think, she's exploring that most basic question whether God exists, and the human instinct to seek help from a transcendent other being, regardless of whether you hold to a formal set of religious beliefs. It is the visceral cry of Jesus on the cross, 'My God, my God.' 'Some days, although we cannot pray, a prayer/utters itself.'

The first stanza depicts a woman in despair who finds a revelatory moment of reprieve in staring 'at the minims sung by a tree.' On the surface this beautiful image doesn't make much sense, but it's a good example of how the poetic voice can produce a line capable of generating a wide range of interpretations. We should never regard poems as riddles to be decoded, otherwise one might as well write in prose in the first place.

The poet suggests there is something, too, about prayer that echoes childhood: learning Latin or to play the piano. The 'Latin chanting of a train' is to me sitting in class 2A reciting dominus, dominus, dominum, domini, domino, domino. I can hear the rhythmic sound of the train's wheels over the joins in the rails. But is this also an implicit criticism of prayer as unthinking repetition of incantations? 'Pray for us now' is an allusion to the *Hail Mary*, a prayer Catholics are often asked to say over and over again, like the imposition of a hundred lines at school, as a penance. 'Holy Mary, Mother of God, pray for us sinners, now and at the hour of our death.'

'Inside the radio's prayer...' is a humorous reference to Radio 4's shipping forecast, of immense value to mariners, and soothing to insomniacs who wake early and can't get back to sleep. Finisterre is of course French for Land's End, or maybe the Biblical 'All the ends of the Earth'. What a pity some jack-in-the-Met-Office decided to change the sea area 'Finisterre' to 'Fitzroy' – the surname given to the illegitimate offspring of kings. There's an added joke though, that not long after the shipping forecast you get 'Prayer for the day', an earnest attempt to relate religion to life, which in some sense is what this poem does. In our devotional recitation of poems on Good Friday it was important to include questioning voices as well as spiritually assured ones because most people interested in developing a personal faith don't want to shy away from the questions religion poses. Questions are productive, not dangerous. The philosopher Blaise Pascal summed this up beautifully in his *Pensées* when he wrote, putting words into the mouth of God, 'You would not seek me if you had not found me.'

–

'Lovest thou me?' by William Cowper (1731-1800)

Hark my soul! it is the Lord;
'Tis Thy Saviour, hear His word;
Jesus speaks and speaks to thee,
"Say poor sinner, lov'st thou me?

"I deliver'd thee when bound,
And when bleeding, heal'd thy wound;
Sought thee wandering, set thee right,
Turn'd thy darkness into light.

"Can a woman's tender care
Cease towards the child she bare?
Yes, she may forgetful be,
Yet will I remember thee.

"Mine is an unchanging love,
Higher than the heights above,
Deeper than the depths beneath,
Free and faithful, strong as death.

"Thou shalt see my glory soon,
When the work of grace is done;
Partner of my throne shalt be;
Say, poor sinner, lov' st thou me?"

Lord it is my chief complaint,
That my love is weak and faint;
Yet I love Thee and adore, --
Oh! for grace to love Thee more!

As a teenager I used to sit in the choir of Loughton Union Church on a Sunday night and listen to tediously long sermons, bible-based but none the better for it. Every now and then there would be relief from the monotony when the preacher stirred the emotions with an appeal to the heart. If ever I were to become a minister, I thought, I'd do this every week. 'Say poor sinner, lov'st thou me?' This poem unashamedly tugs at the heartstrings and now I might accuse it of sentimentality. It pulsates with the evangelical fervour of a poet who twice suffered bouts of madness and came under the evangelical influence of John Newton, the Anglican clergyman and former slave ship master who wrote 'Amazing Grace'.

Its regular metre and rhyming couplets create a mood of puritanical simplicity ('Hark my soul! It is the Lord') as Cowper invents a conversation between Jesus and a sinner who could be of any age and either sex. Jesus is like the Good Samaritan healing the wounds of the injured, his love stronger than the maternal instinct, an unwavering love strong as death. In the fifth stanza, Jesus refers directly to his sacrificial death on the cross as 'the work of grace' which will reveal his glory, and then in the last stanza the sinner responds by pleading guilty to showing only weak love in return. But the last line of the poem, 'Oh! for grace to love Thee more!', sums up the great evangelical, Reformation doctrine of Justification by Faith through grace alone. The idea is that people can be in a right relationship with God, not through any good work or cash payment to the Church, but simply through putting their trust in God. Even that act of faith or trust shows no merit on the part of the believer, but is achieved entirely through God grace.

Well, I do think there's something maudlin in William Cowper's verse, but I have to admit when this poem was read on Good Friday in church it made an impact and resulted in a silence that demanded a response.

Ambulances by Philip Larkin (1922-1985)

Closed like confessionals, they thread
Loud noons of cities, giving back
None of the glances they absorb.
Light glossy grey, arms on a plaque,
They come to rest at any kerb:
All streets in time are visited.

Then children strewn on steps or road,
Or women coming from the shops
Past smells of different dinners, see
A wild white face that overtops
Red stretcher-blankets momently
As it is carried in and stowed,

And sense the solving emptiness
That lies just under all we do,
And for a second get it whole,
So permanent and blank and true.
The fastened doors recede. *Poor soul,*
They whisper at their own distress;

For borne away in deadened air
May go the sudden shut of loss
Round something nearly at an end,
And what cohered in it across
The years, the unique random blend
Of families and fashions, there

At last begin to loosen. Far
From the exchange of love to lie
Unreachable inside a room
The traffic parts to let go by
Brings closer what is left to come,
And dulls to distance all we are.

Philip Larkin once said of himself, 'I'm an agnostic, I suppose, but an Anglican agnostic, of course'. Like many of his contemporaries he wanted to shake off religion but couldn't quite let go. In 'Aubade' he described it as a 'vast, moth-eaten musical brocade / Created to pretend we never die.' 'Ambulances' picks up the theme of death, and the meaning of life, in a cleverly extended image of an ambulance rushing through the city streets, interrupting ordinary people's lunchbreak and midday shopping, to attend a seriously ill patient. The sight of the patient's 'wild white face' above the red blankets on the stretcher sends a momentary shock of mortality through those who see it, so that for a second they 'sense the solving emptiness / That lies just under all we do'. They see themselves in the victim's plight and wonder what it all – 'families and fashions' – adds up to. Everything, from conception, 'the exchange of love', to being confined in the back of this grey 1961 ambulance is suddenly pulled into focus in such a way as questions 'all we are'. There is a sense here too of John Donne: Ask not for whom the ambulance calls, it calls for thee.

To me it's not clear whether this is a totally pessimistic, nihilistic view, suggesting life is devoid of meaning and purpose or whether, in a colourful way, it makes Socrates' claim that an unexamined life is not worth living. The images of 'children strewn on steps', shops, 'smells of different dinners', and 'families and fashions' imply an ordinary, shallow, trivialised existence that begs the question: isn't there more to life than this?

This is the big issue for Good Friday. Surely there is more than this. In contemplating Christ's death one is forced to ask the same questions posed here so arrestingly by Larkin, who is doing an important part of his job as a poet by provoking his readers into thinking for themselves. By contemplating the death of Jesus, a person might be made to think about death itself and whether there is any life or meaning beyond it. We know Christianity replies with a resounding, 'Yes, there is.' The theological term for it is 'eternal' life, which isn't the same as 'everlasting' life. Eternal life is a quality of living based on self-giving, community, consideration for others, and a search for the values that might be considered ultimately important – a life exemplified by Jesus of Nazareth. This kind of reflection would also be the essence of an 'examined life'; and if it has any transcendence – that is to say, if it has potential for meaning beyond the life which spans from conception to that last dash in the back of an ambulance – it is as much potential for the here and now as for the world to come.

Redemption by George Herbert (1593-1633)

Having been tenant long to a rich Lord,
Not thriving, I resolved to be bold,
And make a suit unto him, to afford
A new small-rented lease, and cancel th' old.
In heaven at his manor I him sought:
They told me there, that he was lately gone
About some land, which he had dearly bought
Long since on earth, to take possession.
I straight return'd, and knowing his great birth,
Sought him accordingly in great resorts;
In cities, theatres, gardens, parks, and courts:
At length I heard a ragged noise and mirth
Of thieves and murderers: there I him espied,
Who straight, *Your suit is granted*, said, & died.

On the surface this poem looks straightforward enough: an allegory of a tenant farmer who wants a cheaper, more manageable lease. The farmer is everyman and the modern political equivalent is ubiquitous, whether a family trying to negotiate an affordable rent in London or a shopkeeper in Oxford trying to resist another rent rise imposed by a greedy college. He tries to locate his landlord in the manor house, but learning that the landlord is 'on earth' on business, he naturally searches for him in the 'cities, theatres and gardens' where you'd expect the rich and powerful to hang out, but in the end finds him amongst 'thieves and murderers' – presumably the thieves either side of Christ on the cross and the baying crowd wanting blood. There on Calvary, at the moment he was about to give up the ghost, the landlord (God or Christ) grants the man what he desires – a new lease, better terms, redemption and salvation, a future.

At another level I find the poem difficult. It makes biblical allusions that might have been familiar to the educated readers of Herbert's early-seventeenth-century Salisbury but which are almost totally lost on us today. 'Having been a tenant long to a rich Lord' refers to the Covenant between God and the Israelites, brokered by Moses, when he presented the people with the Ten Commandments. It was sealed in the sacrificial blood of an ox. This was an agreement whereby Israel would keep God's laws and in return God would protect them. The 'new small-rented lease' the farmer was after is what Christians call the 'New Covenant', mentioned every time the priest blesses the wine in the Eucharist: 'this is my blood of the new covenant, which is shed for you and for many for the forgiveness of sins.' In this new agreement God assures people of forgiveness and divine acceptance and in return asks simply for faith.

There's another New Testament echo behind Herbert's poem: the parable of the Wicked Tenants in Matthew 21.33-39 in which a landlord sets up a vineyard, leases it to tenants and moves away to another country. At harvest time he sends his agents to collect the produce, but the tenants kill them. Thinking they'll show more respect he sends his son, but the tenants decide that if they kill the son and heir they'll be able to grab the inheritance for themselves. Herbert doesn't follow this precisely, but in the second stanza God has 'lately gone about some land…to take possession' and, in the final couplet, despite the compression of meaning and description into such a very few words, the son is clearly being killed on the cross amongst thieves and murderers.

The Musician by R.S. Thomas (1913-2000)

A memory of Kreisler once:
At some recital in this same city,
The seats all taken, I found myself pushed
On to the stage with a few others,
So near that I could see the toil
Of his face muscles, a pulse like a moth
Fluttering under the fine skin,
And the indelible veins of his smooth brow.

I could see, too, the twitching of the fingers,
Caught temporarily in art's neurosis,
As we sat there or warmly applauded
This player who so beautifully suffered
For each of us upon his instrument.

So it must have been on Calvary
In the fiercer light of the thorns' halo:
The men standing by and that one figure,
The hands bleeding, the mind bruised but calm,
Making such music as lives still.
And no one daring to interrupt
Because it was himself that he played
And closer than all of them the God listened.

Of all the poems in this selection 'The Musician' is the one I return to most often. I once had the privilege of hosting the great cellist, Paul Tortelier, who had come to Oxford for a few days to give a masterclass. I couldn't help noticing the calluses on the fingertips of his left hand, like the pads of a dog's paw, hardened by six hours' practice a day, and how he hung by his fingers from the door frame of our living room to stretch his back, strained by years of playing. And then, in performance, we saw from the front row the extortions of his face and the sweat on his cheeks as he brought to life so much more music than was written on the page. He had seemed so vibrant, larger than life, telling his pupils they must not try to be purists but must be free, and then a month later he had died of a heart attack in his home country, France.

RS Thomas doesn't make the mistake of trivialising or romanticising the crucifixion by equating it with the privileged delight of the concert hall. Hence the separateness of the last stanza which sets the crucifixion in a different category of physical experience. But the image of Christ as an artist who discovers new meaning and creativity through a life of disciplined self-giving is a powerful one for me.

The last line has puzzled me. Why the definite article before God, as if this is one of many gods, even though God is capitalised? It seems to put God at a distance despite the word 'closer' in the same sentence. Then I notice that God is more attentive than anyone else in the audience, rapt in concentration though they are. And somehow this very faith-questioning poet has suggested that in the crucifixion humans are brought close to the essence of depth and meaning.

Interestingly, George Herbert used the same musical image three hundred years earlier when he wrote of Christ in his poem 'Easter':

Awake, my lute, and struggle for thy part
With all thy art.
The crosse taught all wood to resound his name

Who bore the same.
His stretched sinews taught all strings, what key
Is best to celebrate this most high day...

Herbert suggests the wood of the cross is like a sounding board which shouts out the Name of Jesus Christ just as a lute or violin uses a wooden sound box to amplify the sound of vibrating strings. Playing further with the image, and with a pun on the word 'taught' (taut), he says the stretched sinews of Christ's crucified body are like the gut strings of all stringed instruments. It is almost certain that RS Thomas was familiar with this poem of Herbert's.

The Crown of Thorns 13th century; tr Athelstan Riley (1858-1945)

Dost thou truly seek renown
Christ his glory sharing?
Wouldst thou win the heavenly crown
Victor's garland bearing?
Tread the path the Saviour trod,
Look upon the crown of God,
See what he is wearing.

This the King of Heaven bore
In that sore contending;
This His sacred temples wore,
Honour to it lending;
In this helmet faced the foe,
On the rood he laid him low,
Satan's kingdom ending.

Christ upon the tree of scorn,
In salvation's hour,
Turned to gold those pricks of thorn
By his passion's power;
So on sinners, who had earned
Endless death, from sin returned,
Endless blessings shower.

When in death's embrace we lie,
Then, good Lord, be near us;
With thy presence fortify,
And with victory cheer us;
Turn our erring hearts to Thee,
That we crowned for ay may be:
O good Jesu, hear us!

Athelstan Riley was a hymn-writer and translator who chaired the editorial board of the *English Hymnal*, published in 1906, edited by Percy Dearmer and Ralph Vaughan Williams and used primarily by the Anglo-Catholic wing of the Church of England. Riley's best known hymn is 'Ye Watchers and Ye Holy Ones', calling on the saints and apostles to lead a flash-mob dance in heaven to the strains of 'Alleluia'.

'Dost thou truly seek renown' appears as hymn 81 in the *New English Hymnal*, but I had never sung it or been inclined to select it for a Holy Week service. However, the backcloth for the public reading of these poems on Good Friday in the University Church was always a life-sized wooden cross placed where the nave altar would normally stand, with a crown, woven from a viciously sharp thorn bush in the University Parks, hung on a nail just where the head of Christ would have been. It was a powerful symbol made all the more potent having cut the thorns myself and in the process of plaiting them realising the cruel cynicism of the soldiers who pressed such a crown onto the head of Jesus. To mock a condemned man is as cold-blooded as to hammer the nails through his hands and feet.

While this poem veers towards sentimentality it seems to me to explore the image of the crown of thorns in such a way as to add to the spiritual contemplation of the cross.

Christians and Pagans by Dietrich Bonhoeffer (1906-1945)

People turn to God when they're in need,
plead for help, contentment, and for bread,
for rescue from their sickness, guilt, and death.
They all do so, both Christian and pagan.

People turn to God in God's own need,
and find God poor, degraded, without roof or bread,
see God devoured by sin, weakness, and death.
Christians stand with God to share God's pain.

God turns to all people in their need,
nourishes body and soul with God's own bread,
takes up the cross for Christians and pagans, both,
and in forgiving both, is slain.

This poem scarcely needs any explanation. What you see is what you get – an honest to goodness statement that many people experience an instinctive need for God; a need partly satisfied by an empathy with Christ's humble, self-denying life and admiring him for it, which all leads to a picture of God as inclusive, accepting everyone whatever their religious affiliation. So the title is important: God is not for the exclusive use of Christians. God is for Christians and Pagans alike.

To understand how Dietrich Bonhoeffer reaches this refreshingly open view it's useful to see his life in context. Apart from being one of the best theologians of his generation he was also one of the bravest, publicly opposing Nazism and plotting with others the downfall of Hitler, for which he was hanged at Flossenbürg in 1945, three weeks before the end of the war. Acutely aware of the Church's failure to oppose the Nazi persecution, he saw Christianity as trapped in religious institutionalism and defined by elitist metaphysical beliefs. He questioned the meaning of God and Christ for the contemporary world and argued for a new approach for which he coined the phrase 'religionless Christianity'. He didn't mean that God was dead, but that God must be understood in different terms. Hitherto, it seemed to him, God had been located in a distant metaphysical world, in the shrinking area of unsolved problems as yet unexplained by science, and in the shrouded recesses of mysticism. People say that God can only be known in Jesus Christ, but who is Christ for us today, asks Bonhoeffer. In a famous phrase he said, 'God is the beyond in the midst of our lives'. That is, God is not only the transcendent other; God is the arresting, surprising, counter-cultural shock of meaning that occasionally jumps out at us in various unexpected ways. He also said, 'God lets himself be pushed out of the world onto the cross', which must have echoed his own experience of being imprisoned, knowing the most likely outcome would be execution. In such apocalyptic personal circumstances one's mind is bound to cut to the chase and see through any hypocrisy or theological double-talk.

Friday's Child WH Auden (1907-73)
(in memory of Dietrich Bonhoeffer, martyred at Flossenbürg,
April 9, 1945)

He told us we were free to choose
But, children as we were, we thought—
"Paternal Love will only use
Force in the last resort

On those too bumptious to repent."
Accustomed to religious dread,
It never crossed our minds He meant
Exactly what He said.

Perhaps He frowns, perhaps He grieves,
But it seems idle to discuss
If anger or compassion leaves
The bigger bangs to us.

What reverence is rightly paid
To a Divinity so odd
He lets the Adam whom He made
Perform the Acts of God?

It might be jolly if we felt
Awe at this Universal Man
(When kings were local, people knelt);
Some try to, but who can?

The self-observed observing Mind
We meet when we observe at all
Is not alarming or unkind
But utterly banal.

Though instruments at Its command
Make wish and counterwish come true,

It clearly cannot understand
What It can clearly do.

Since the analogies are rot
Our senses based belief upon,
We have no means of learning what
Is really going on,

And must put up with having learned
All proofs or disproofs that we tender
Of His existence are returned
Unopened to the sender.

Now, did He really break the seal
And rise again? We dare not say;
But conscious unbelievers feel
Quite sure of Judgement Day.

Meanwhile, a silence on the cross,
As dead as we shall ever be,
Speaks of some total gain or loss,
And you and I are free

To guess from the insulted face
Just what Appearances He saves
By suffering in a public place
A death reserved for slaves.

Like so much of Auden this is difficult to paraphrase and it's not altogether obvious quite how it relates to Dietrich Bonhoeffer except to say according to the nursery rhyme, 'Friday's child is loving and giving'; and in a sense that could apply to Bonhoeffer's martyrdom, even if not to the same degree as it could be said of Good Friday and Christ on the cross.

With a wit and scepticism typical of Auden, the first three stanzas discuss the notion that God gave humans free will to choose between right and wrong. The fourth puts the problem of evil in a nutshell: what god worth his salt allows the fallen 'Adam whom he made / Perform the acts of God?' This might remind us of some contemporary politicians.

In the eighth and ninth stanzas, vain attempts to prove the existence of God are mocked as having to be 'returned to sender' – or, as we might say, not fit for purpose. In verse five the idiomatic 'It might be jolly if we felt / Awe at this Universal Man' suggests standing lightly towards pompous theology.

Having ridiculed theology's failure to wrap up its case for Christianity, the poem brings us finally to an awe-struck silence in face of the cross and an evil that cannot be understood – both Christ's silence in death and our gasp of silence in response as we apprehend 'some total loss or gain', some absolute, ultimate significance here. Yet the meaning lies not in any certainty but in our freedom to respond to the 'insulted face' of Christ. In a sense these final lines are qualified with the earlier question whether Christ really rose from the tomb. 'We dare not say'. But amid all the ambiguity and uncertainty the story of the Passion still provokes a faith that, as Kierkegaard said, can be neither explained nor justified.

At a Calvary near the Ancre Wilfred Owen (1893-1918)

One ever hangs where shelled roads part.
In this war He too lost a limb,
But His disciples hide apart;
And now the Soldiers bear with Him.

Near Golgotha strolls many a priest,
And in their faces there is pride
That they were flesh-marked by the Beast
By whom the gentle Christ's denied.

The scribes on all the people shove
And bawl allegiance to the state,
But they who love the greater love
Lay down their life; they do not hate.

Wilfred Owen was arguably the greatest of the First World War poets and, along with Siegfried Sassoon, one of its loudest critics. In the draft introduction to his posthumously published single volume of poetry he had written, 'Above all I am not concerned with Poetry. My subject is War, and the pity of War. The Poetry is in the pity.'

In this poem he sees a roadside crucifix, such as there are in many a French village, damaged by shellfire and, like so many soldiers in battle, having lost a leg. So here's a parallel between the suffering of Christ's crucifixion and the dreadful wounds of soldiers who were described by some as 'cannon fodder'.

The priests who stroll by and the scribes who 'bawl allegiance to the state' remind us of the priest and Levite who passed by on the other side of the road from the man who fell among thieves in the story of the *Good Samaritan*. For Owen they are perhaps the officers. Whereas the ordinary soldiers being killed in the trenches show the 'greater love' spoken of by Jesus when he said, 'Greater love has no one than this, than to lay down one's life for one's friends.'

The puzzling line about the mark of the beast refers to the Book of Revelation (14:10): 'If anyone worships the beast and his image and receives his mark on the forehead or on the hand, he, too, will drink of the wine of God's fury.' The beast is the devil and those who show this pride in war and indifference to its suffering are about the devil's work.

The 'War that was to end all Wars' was so outrageously wasteful of human lives that it produced a crisis of conscience for Western society, and in religion a challenge to belief in the existence of God itself. How could a loving and just God allow suffering on such an industrial scale?

The Explosion Philip Larkin (1922-1985)

On the day of the explosion
Shadows pointed towards the pithead:
In the sun the slagheap slept.

Down the lane came men in pitboots
Coughing oath-edged talk and pipe-smoke,
Shouldering off the freshened silence.

One chased after rabbits; lost them;
Came back with a nest of lark's eggs;
Showed them; lodged them in the grasses.

So they passed in beards and moleskins,
Fathers, brothers, nicknames, laughter,
Through the tall gates standing open.

At noon there came a tremor; cows
Stopped chewing for a second; sun
Scarfed as in a heat-haze dimmed.

The dead go on before us, they
Are sitting in God's house in comfort,
We shall see them face to face —

plain as lettering in the chapels
It was said, and for a second
Wives saw men of the explosion

Larger than in life they managed —
Gold as on a coin, or walking
Somehow from the sun towards them

One showing the eggs unbroken.

Philip Larkin has a famously bleak outlook on life, if often softened with humour. We see it in 'Mr Bleaney', trapped in a grim bedsit; or in 'I Remember, I Remember' in which Larkin deprecates his home town of Coventry, where his 'childhood was unspent'. But 'The Explosion' strikes a more positive note, even as he describes the subterranean devastation and tragic fallout of a coal mining disaster. Despite the ominous shadows pointing to the pithead, the miners bowl happily along to work swearing and laughing, one hiding some larks' eggs in the grass to collect on the way home. With an arresting reference to the crucifixion, at noon there's a tremor and the sun dims. We read in Matthew 27 verses 45 and 52: 'From noon on, darkness came over the whole land until three in the afternoon. And about three o'clock Jesus cried with a loud voice... At that moment... the earth shook, and the rocks were split.' In the simple line, 'cows / stopped chewing for a second' Larkin indicates Nature's indifference to human suffering.

The next stanza, written in italics, appears like a memorial inscription on a church wall and morphs into what appears to be the subsequent memorial service...

'One showing the eggs unbroken' reminds us of new life and possibly of Easter. Larkin was too much of a 'Christian atheist' to go straight for the resurrection, and almost certainly reluctant to suggest any sense of false consolation. That was definitely not up his street and I applaud him for that.

Anthem Leonard Cohen (1934-2016)

The birds they sang
at the break of day
Start again,
I heard them say,
Don't dwell on what
has passed away
or what is yet to be.
The wars they will
be fought again
The holy dove
be caught again
bought and sold
and bought again;
the dove is never free.

Ring the bells that still can ring.
Forget your perfect offering.
There is a crack in everything.
That's how the light gets in.

We asked for signs
the signs were sent:
the birth betrayed,
the marriage spent;
the widowhood
of every government –
signs for all to see.
Can't run no more
with that lawless crowd
while the killers in high places
say their prayers out loud.
But they've summoned up
a thundercloud.
They're going to hear from me.

Ring the bells that still can ring.
Forget your perfect offering.
There is a crack in everything.
That's how the light gets in.

You can add up the parts
but you won't have the sum
You can strike up the march,
there is no drum.
Every heart
to love will come
but like a refugee.

Ring the bells that still can ring.
Forget your perfect offering.
There is a crack in everything.
That's how the light gets in.

Even I am wondering what this one is doing here — both in terms of its relation to my theme and the quality of its verse. I bought a copy of Leonard Cohen's poems in 1976 on the recommendation of an undergraduate and read them with passing interest when I was helping run a poetry class which met in my rooms in Sidney Sussex College. Snootily I assumed a song writer couldn't be a literary figure. Little did I guess that one day Bob Dylan would win the Nobel Prize for Literature.

It's the refrain that works for me. 'Ring the bells that still can ring. Forget your perfect offering. There's a crack in everything. That's how the light gets in.' Writing in the *Independent* some years back, Howard Jacobson said the words had the same effect on him. 'Could he be singing this to me? You expect too much, mister. You are too unforgiving. Not everything works out, not everything is great, and not everyone must like what you like.' There's a crack in everything. Jacobson again: 'And then comes another, still more wonderful, clinching line – "That's how the light gets in." Savour that! At a stroke, weakness becomes strength and fault becomes virtue.' I get the point.

Christianity makes a lot of perfection: perfect God and perfect man, be perfect as your heavenly Father is perfect. God is omni this and omni that and is immutable because that which is perfect can never change. But the flaws of heavenly perfection have often been pointed out: a golfer always gets round in eighteen, Tottenham Hotspur always win the Premier League, your cooking, and your enjoyment of it, can never get better. So life is dull because, in reality, good days are defined by off days, and joy is sharpened by sorrow. In the perfect world even scholarship and learning brings no satisfaction because everything is known and there's nothing to learn.

In the story of the perfect God/Man, Jesus, the illuminating moments are of vulnerability, it seems to me: turning over the tables of the money-changers in the temple, the prayer in Gethsemane, 'If it be your will take this cup from me', Peter's denial, Judas' betrayal, Jesus' fall as he carries his cross along the *Via Dolorosa*, his cry of god-forsakenness from the cross. If we really took this perfection seriously and salvation was effected by some sort of superman it wouldn't have the same power. In a wonderful poem by Christopher Smart, *The Nativity of our Lord and Saviour Jesus Christ*, there's a verse:

'O the magnitude of meekness!
Worth from worth immortal sprung;
O the strength of infant weakness,
If eternal is so young!'

There's a crack in everything. That's how the light get in.

Woefully Arrayed John Skelton (1460?-1529)

Woefully arrayed,
My blood, man,
For thee ran,
It may not be nayed:
My body blue and wan,
Woefully arrayed.

Behold me, I pray thee, with all thine whole reason,
And be not hard-hearted for this encheason,   (*cause*)
That I for thy soul's sake was slain in good season,
Beguiled and betrayed by Judas' false treason:
Unkindly entreated,
With sharp cords sore fretted, (*gashed across the back*)
The Jewes me threated:
They mowed, they grinned, they scorned me   (*grimaced*)
Condemned to death, as thou mayest see,
Woefully arrayed.

Thus naked am I nailed, O man, for thy sake!
I love thee, then love me; why sleepst thou? awake!
Remember my tender heart-root for thee brake,
With pains my veins constrained to crack:
Thus tugged to and fro,
Thus wrapped all in woe,
Whereas never man was so,
Entreated thus in most cruel wise,
Was like a lamb offered in sacrifice,
Woefully arrayed.

Of sharp thorn I have worn a crown on my head,
So pained, so strained, so rueful, so red,
Thus bobbed, thus robbed, thus for thy love dead,   (*struck*)
Unfeigned I deigned my blood for to shed:
My feet and hands sore

The sturdy nails bore:
What might I suffer more
Than I have done, O man, for thee?
Come when thou list, welcome to me,
Woefully arrayed.

Of record thy good Lord I have been and shall be:
I am thine, thou art mine, my brother I call thee.
Thee love I entirely—see what is befall'n me!
Sore beating, sore threating, to make thee, man, all free:
Why art thou unkind?
Why hast not me in mind?
Come yet and thou shalt find
Mine endless mercy and grace—
See how a spear my heart did race,   (*pierce*)
Woefully arrayed.

Dear brother, no other thing I of thee desire
But give me thine heart free to reward mine hire:
I wrought thee, I bought thee from eternal fire:
I pray thee array thee toward my high empire
Above the orient,
Whereof I am regent,
Lord God omnipotent,
With me to reign in endless wealth:
Remember, man, thy soul's health.

Woefully arrayed,
My blood, man,
For thee ran,
It may not be nayed:
My body blue and wan,
Woefully arrayed.

[From the Fairfax MS. (which once belonged to Ralph Thoresby, and now forms part of the Additional MSS., 5465, in the British Museum), where it occurs twice (fol. 76 and, less perfectly, fol. 86); collated with a copy written in a very old hand on the flyleaves of Boetius de Discip. Schol. cum notabili commento, Daventrie, 1496, 4to. (in the collection of the late Mr. Heber), which has supplied several stanzas not in the Fairfax MS. It was printed from the latter, not very correctly, by Sir John Hawkins, Hist. of Music, ii. 89.]

Back in the early Seventies at Christ Church, Lancaster Gate on the North side of Kensington Gardens, we used to hold an annual 'Passiontide Carol Service' in an attempt to attract the kind of crowd for Easter that you could so easily draw for Christmas. To add spice to the mix we persuaded some famous people to read. The actor, Frank Windsor, Detective Sergeant John Watt in BBC TV's *Z-Cars* from 1962-65 was one, and Peter Jeffrey who played the headmaster in the film *If* was another. Peter, who had been at Harrow with the vicar, read 'Woefully Arrayed'. Hearing him read showed how a good actor could make the repetition of 'woefully arrayed' at the end of each stanza subtly different, nuanced with a varied intonation.

The poem creates much of its intensity from the urgent, insistent rhythm and patterned rhyme scheme, but also from the in-your-face realism of its portrayal of the violence of crucifixion: Jesus' back cut like a fretwork by thirty-nine lashes and his cry, 'thus naked am I nailed', with 'sturdy' nails until his body is 'blue and wan'. After centuries of Christian reflection on the meaning of Christ's death, the dreadful reality of a Roman execution is sometimes lost behind the theology of redemption, salvation and triumph over death. There's an ever-present danger of romanticising Good Friday, only to be brought back to earth, say, by the spine-chilling report of a contemporary crucifixion perpetrated by ISIL in Syria, when all the nauseating horror of it comes home.

Having set that scene, the poet calls for a moral and emotional response from the reader: 'I love thee, then love me.' 'No other thing I of thee desire / But give me thine heart.' Let's assume Skelton wrote it: maybe he was, as Stanley Fish suggests, influenced stylistically by the *Reproaches*, sung during the Veneration of the Cross as part of the Catholic liturgy for Good Friday. In these responses Jesus lists some of the good things God has done for his people, but their response is to crucify him.

'O my people what have I done to you? Or wherein have I wearied you? Answer me.
I led you forth from the land of Egypt,
and delivered you by the waters of baptism,
but you have prepared a cross for your Saviour.'

from **The York Pageant of the Pinners and Painters:**
The Crucifixion (mid-15th century)

2 SOLDIER
Now since we four shall do this deed,
And meddle with this unthrifty thing,
Let no man spare for special speed,
Till that we have made ending.

3 SOLDIER
This work we may not fail;
Now we are right arrayed.

4 SOLDIER
This boy here in our bail
Shall bide full bitter braid.

1 SOLDIER
Sir knights, say now, work we ought?

2 SOLDIER
Yes, certainly, I've got hold this hand.

3 SOLDIER
And to the bore I have it brought
Full buxomly without a band.

1 SOLDIER
Strike on then hard, by Him thee bought.

2 SOLDIER
This nail, I think, will stiffly stand;
Through bones and sinews it shall be sought.
I guarantee this work is good.

1 SOLDIER
Say, Sir, how do we there?
This business cannot be delayed.

3 SOLDIER:
His arm's a foot short or more;
His sinews must have shrunk.

4 SOLDIER:
Perhaps the holes were bored too wide.

2 SOLDIER:
Then he'll endure some bitter bale!

3 SOLDIER:
In faith, the measurements are wrongly scored;
That's why the hole is bound to fail.

1 SOLDIER:
Why carp ye so? Fasten on a cord,
And stretch his arms until they reach.

3 SOLDIER:
Yea, thou commandest lightly as a lord;
Come, help to pull him; one arm each.

1 SOLDIER:
Certainly, that shall I do –
Full quickly as a snail.

3 SOLDIER:
And I'll attach him to,
Full nimbly with a nail.

This work will hold; that dare I heet,
(*promise*)

For now are fastened both his hands.

4 SOLDIER:
Go we all four, then, to his feet;
So our time is quickly spent.

2 SOLDIER:
Let's see what jest might make pain sweet;
Thereto, my back now I would bend.

The language and vocabulary of fifteenth-century York, where this mystery play originates, is not at all accessible to the modern ear and therefore, in adapting this short extract, I have partly drawn on *Everyman and Medieval Miracle Plays* (ed. A.C. Cawley) and a translation by Chester N. Scoville and Kimberley M. Yates, Toronto, 2003. I have tried to preserve something of the idiom and rhythm of the original but have given priority to a text that should be immediately understood.

The medieval mystery plays which developed in cities such as York, Wakefield, Chester and Coventry were performed on carts in the streets and were a way of bringing biblical stories to the common people who wouldn't have understood the Latin used in church services. They were sponsored by craft guilds and acted by different tradesmen according to their theme, so that the building of Noah's Ark might be performed by the shipwrights, the Last Supper by the Bakers, the Adoration of the Magi by the Goldsmiths, and, in this case, the Crucifixion by the Pinners and Painters.

What this extract adds to the overall theme of this anthology is a view from the perspective of Jesus' executioners. Were they indifferent to the suffering of their victims? Did they see it as all in a day's work? They recognise their victim is going to suffer terribly, but they have a job to do, and since the carpenter who made the cross has drilled the holes for the nails in the wrong place, they are absorbed with stretching the body to accommodate the error regardless of the added cruelty. This reveals a fact about human behaviour described as 'the banality of evil' by Hannah Arendt when she was covering the trial of Adolph Eichmann, who masterminded the systematic extermination of Jews in World War II. She didn't mean the crime against humanity was banal in the sense of being of little importance, but that it became routine, systematic, and everyday for those who implemented it, and from the philosophical point of view morally unreflected upon.

Psychologically, it seems to me, we cannot bear much suffering and therefore, if we can, shut it out, as most people do when watching news reports of atrocities around the world. It is likely then that torturers, especially those who are agents for state authority, as the Romans soldiers were, need to acquire insensitivity towards their victims in order to remain sane. But they are not altogether morally indifferent and will make a judgement as to whether they think the victim deserves the punishment or not. Yet, whether state-authorised or terrorist, the torturers will know that if they fail in their task they themselves will be tortured, hence they manage by seeing their task as no more than a job that they have to do. The character of the action is caught somewhere between banality and the vicious circle of evil. Psychology might not really have got off the ground until the nineteenth century, but the medieval playwright has real insight into the question of evil.

Friday Elizabeth Jennings (1926-2001)

We nailed the hands long ago,
Wove the thorns, took up the scourge and shouted
For excitement's sake, we stood at the dusty edge
Of the pebbled path and watched the extreme of pain.

But one or two prayed, one or two
Were silent, shocked, stood back
And remembered remnants of words, a new vision,
The cross is up with its crying victim, the clouds
Cover the sun, we learn a new way to lose
What we did not know we had
Until this bleak and sacrificial day,
Until we turned from our bad
Past and knelt and cried out our dismay,
The dice still clicking, the voices dying away.

Although born in Lincolnshire, Elizabeth Jennings was very much an Oxford poet, having lived there from the age of six and studied at St Anne's College before working as a librarian at the Oxford City Library. She was a devout Roman Catholic, and religion is an important theme in much of her work, along with love and death.

The voice of this poem in the first person plural implicates the reader in the action – 'we nailed the hands' – and echoes the question of the Negro spiritual, 'Were you there when they crucified my Lord?' Her description is simple and assured, 'we stood at the dusty edge / of the pebbled path'. But what is 'our' response? Mixed: prayer, shock, and recollection of some of the things he said. Then there is the puzzling 'we learn a new way to lose / What we did not know we had', and the ending where repentance seems the solution, despite the fact human corruption persists, represented by the soldiers' dice still clicking, and that the galvanising moral urgency of the 'crying victim' fades away in the memory.

When I survey the wondrous cross Isaac Watts (1674-1748)

When I survey the wondrous cross
On which the Prince of glory died,
My richest gain I count but loss,
And pour contempt on all my pride.

Forbid it, Lord, that I should boast,
Save in the death of Christ my God!
All the vain things that charm me most,
I sacrifice them to His blood.

See from His head, His hands, His feet,
Sorrow and love flow mingled down!
Did e'er such love and sorrow meet,
Or thorns compose so rich a crown?

His dying crimson, like a robe,
Spreads o'er His body on the tree;
Then I am dead to all the globe,
And all the globe is dead to me.

Were the whole realm of nature mine,
That were a present far too small;
Love so amazing, so divine,
Demands my soul, my life, my all.

Perhaps the best known of the Passiontide hymns, this poem by Isaac Watts has much in common with 'Woefully Arrayed', particularly in the third stanza referring to the physical suffering of crucifixion. But there's a sense of being once-removed from the reality by an excursion into romantic theology: Christ's blood is 'like a robe', 'sorrow and love flow mingled down' from the suppurating wounds in his hands and feet, 'sorrow' surely not nearly strong enough a word. We sing it with a sense of warm devotion and a degree of satisfaction. But the challenge we saw in 'Woefully Arrayed' and the *Reproaches* is there: imagining the cross (which has become 'wondrous') one is pushed towards contempt for pride; and, in the final couplet, Jesus' death and the manner of it demands a life-changing response – 'my soul, my life, my all.'

When a text is known more by the singing of it than by the reading of it, the music adds an interpretation that can go sneakily unnoticed. The eighteenth century tune, *Rockingham*, which normally accompanies it, has an emotive melody and a similarly affecting harmonisation (from Webbe's *Collection of Psalm Tunes 1820*) so when the poem is read out loud it carries a range of different emphases.

And Death Shall Have No Dominion Dylan Thomas (1914-53)

And death shall have no dominion.
Dead men naked they shall be one
With the man in the wind and the west moon;
When their bones are picked clean and the clean bones gone,
They shall have stars at elbow and foot;
Though they go mad they shall be sane,
Though they sink through the sea they shall rise again;
Though lovers be lost love shall not;
And death shall have no dominion.

And death shall have no dominion.
Under the windings of the sea
They lying long shall not die windily;
Twisting on racks when sinews give way,
Strapped to a wheel, yet they shall not break;
Faith in their hands shall snap in two,
And the unicorn evils run them through;
Split all ends up they shan't crack;
And death shall have no dominion.

And death shall have no dominion.
No more may gulls cry at their ears
Or waves break loud on the seashores;
Where blew a flower may a flower no more
Lift its head to the blows of the rain;
Though they be mad and dead as nails,
Heads of the characters hammer through daisies;
Break in the sun till the sun breaks down,
And death shall have no dominion.

The resonance of this great declaratory poem is captured perfectly in the silky-rough, musical voice of Richard Burton which can still be heard in an old recording widely available on the internet. It picks up a triumphant passage from St Paul in Romans 6.9-10 about Christ's victory over death: 'We know that Christ, being raised from the dead, will never die again; death no longer has dominion over him. The death he died, he died to sin, once for all; but the life he lives, he lives to God.' At the beginning and end of each stanza the proclamation of resilient life rings out like a rousing political speech – Martin Luther King's 'I have a dream' speech, for example. It is heroic and emotional. It shows all the rhetorical love of words characteristic of Dylan Thomas, but the imagery is straightforward: the mad will be sane, the dead and the drowned will rise, the tortured will not crack, and those in the tombs, rather than kicking up daisies, will smash up through the ground with their heads. The only quirky play with imagery is in line three where one might expect 'the man in the moon and the west wind', but moon needs to be at the end of the line to rhyme with 'one' and 'gone'.

The Road Not Taken Robert Frost (1874-1963)

Two roads diverged in a yellow wood,
And sorry I could not travel both
And be one traveler, long I stood
And looked down one as far as I could
To where it bent in the undergrowth;

Then took the other, as just as fair,
And having perhaps the better claim
Because it was grassy and wanted wear,
Though as for that the passing there
Had worn them really about the same,

And both that morning equally lay
In leaves no step had trodden black.
Oh, I kept the first for another day!
Yet knowing how way leads on to way
I doubted if I should ever come back.

I shall be telling this with a sigh
Somewhere ages and ages hence:
Two roads diverged in a wood, and I,
I took the one less traveled by,
And that has made all the difference.

It was the teenagers themselves who wanted to include this one, having, I suppose, studied it at school or heard it cited in an end-of-year valedictory address about going out into the world and taking your chances. If it is relevant here, it's because it highlights the predicament of having to face up to major choices in life when the options look equally balanced. In the events leading up to the crucifixion not enough consideration is given to the dilemma Jesus faced when he prayed, 'Father, if it be your will take this cup from me.' In other words, torture and death were not his number one choice. He needn't have gone to Jerusalem at all, but could have remained in the comparative obscurity of Galilee; although John the Baptist hadn't fared any better in Galilee, ending up with his head on a plate at the behest of Herod's wife, cut off by the officers of Herod Antipas – the same man, according to Luke, involved in Jesus' trial. Jesus appears before Herod who fails to find him guilty, mocks him, and sends him back to Pilate.

The alternative take is that Jesus never had a choice: either because he was sent by God to do a job which included dying for the sins of the world; or, to put it another way, because he *was* God and the saving act of his death was part of his divine plan. Or because, despite the natural human survival instinct, Jesus submitted absolutely to his Father's will. A theologian might say Jesus wouldn't have been human if he hadn't trembled at the prospect of death, and wouldn't have been God if he hadn't have gone through with it. It opens up the question that has occupied Christians for two thousand years: in what sense was Christ human, and in what sense divine.

But did he take 'the road less travelled'? In the poem the two paths lay equally 'in leaves no step had trodden black.' And while the road to martyrdom is in one sense obviously less travelled, the quandary posed in the poem is an enigmatic one. In Martin Scorsese's *The Last Temptation of Christ* Jesus hallucinates on the cross and imagines a quiet domestic life married to Mary Magdalen, bringing up their children together. There were alternatives.

Having said that, we know Frost's poem was intended partly as a joke in which he wished to say the chosen path really is of little consequence, and you end up where you're going anyway. In one sense this is obviously true, like the horrible cliché 'we are where we are', but it doesn't invalidate the interpretation that many readers have put on this poem that it explores the experience of choice and dilemma and our responsibility for making decisions.

Greater Love Wilfred Owen (1893-1918)

Red lips are not so red
As the stained stones kissed by the English dead.
Kindness of wooed and wooer
Seems shame to their love pure.
O Love, your eyes lose lure
When I behold eyes blinded in my stead!

Your slender attitude
Trembles not exquisite like limbs knife-skewed,
Rolling and rolling there
Where God seems not to care:
Till the fierce love they bear
Cramps them in death's extreme decrepitude.

Your voice sings not so soft, —
Though even as wind murmuring through raftered loft, —
Your dear voice is not dear,
Gentle, and evening clear,
As theirs whom none now hear,
Now earth has stopped their piteous mouths that coughed.

Heart, you were never hot
Nor large, nor full like hearts made great with shot;
And though your hand be pale,
Paler are all which trail
Your cross through flame and hail:
Weep, you may weep, for you may touch them not.

Here is Wilfred Owen again with a polemical tour de force on love. The title alludes directly to Jesus' words in St John's Gospel (15.13), 'Greater love hath no man than this, that a man lay down his life for his friends.' But the opening line pictures a Forces' sweetheart, dolled up with red lipstick – self-sacrificial love versus romantic love, a love which by contrast with the suffering of the soldiers seems to the poet second rate. At the beginning of each stanza he adds more brush strokes to his portrait of the girlfriend, fiancée, or wife at home: red lips, slender attitude, soft voice, hot heart.

This gap between *eros* and *agape*, romance and sacrifice, highlights the tragedy of war. Young people, in the springtime of their lives, should be enjoying romance and marriage, not separation and death, and for many of the men a miserable death in God-forsaken circumstances.

The poem is impassioned, overdone, even a little gauche. But here is the protesting anger of a young officer sickened by the futility of war, bursting with emotion and righteous indignation.

The Hippopotamus TS Eliot (1888-1965)

The broad-backed hippopotamus
Rests on his belly in the mud;
Although he seems so firm to us
He is merely flesh and blood.

Flesh-and-blood is weak and frail,
Susceptible to nervous shock;
While the True Church can never fail
For it is based upon a rock.

The hippo's feeble steps may err
In compassing material ends,
While the True Church need never stir
To gather in its dividends.

The 'potamus can never reach
The mango on the mango-tree;
But fruits of pomegranate and peach
Refresh the Church from over sea.

At mating time the hippo's voice
Betrays inflexions hoarse and odd,
But every week we hear rejoice
The Church, at being one with God.

The hippopotamus's day
Is passed in sleep; at night he hunts;
God works in a mysterious way—
The Church can sleep and feed at once.

I saw the 'potamus take wing
Ascending from the damp savannas,
And quiring angels round him sing
The praise of God, in loud hosannas.

Blood of the Lamb shall wash him clean
And him shall heavenly arms enfold,
Among the saints he shall be seen
Performing on a harp of gold.

He shall be washed as white as snow,
By all the martyr'd virgins kist,
While the True Church remains below
Wrapt in the old miasmal mist.

Ungainly and doleful, the hippopotamus is the butt of some sardonic humour, as in Flanders and Swann's eponymous song:

'A regular army of hippopotami
All singing this haunting refrain:
Mud, mud glorious mud,
Nothing quite like it for cooling the blood.
So follow me follow,
Down to the hollow,
And there let us wallow in glorious mud.'

Eliot picks up a similar absurdity with this witty spoof contrasting the Church with a hippopotamus. The hippo might look like an island in the water but it's only flesh and blood, weak and frail, whereas the Church is built on the rock which is Jesus. The hippo struggles for material survival; the church has a massive investment portfolio. The hippo cannot reach the mangos on the mango tree; the church eats exotic fruit from its commonwealth branches overseas. You might say the Church cannot see the wood for the trees and so, while the cumbersome hippo sails off to heaven accompanied by angel choirs, the Church remains, fog-bound, on the ground. It's an observation others have made. Philip Pullman entitled a book *The Good Jesus and the Scoundrel Christ,* making a distinction between the self-denyingly good life of Jesus of Nazareth as presented in the gospels and the flawed and divided organisation, founded by St Paul, which grew into the land-owning, king-making power-structure known as the Western Church. T S Eliot was a devout high churchman whose later poetry, such as *Ash Wednesday* and the *Four Quartets,* explores in depth the themes of meaning, time, God, and personal devotion : he is not mocking but making the prophetic point that organised religion must keep in touch with its roots in the ministry of Jesus. And there is no more rooted, no more radical, day than Good Friday, where one sees true goodness in the suffering of one man made totally desolate by sticking to his beliefs and his sense of what is right and wrong.

from **Meditation 17** John Donne (1572-1631)

Perchance he for whom this bell tolls may be so ill as that he knows not it tolls for him. And perchance I may think myself so much better than I am, as that they who are about me, and see my state, may have caused it to toll for me, and I know not that. The church is catholic, universal, so are all her actions; all that she does, belongs to all. When she baptizes a child, that action concerns me; for that child is thereby connected to that head which is my head too, and ingraffed into that body, whereof I am a member. And when she buries a man, that action concerns me; all mankind is of one author, and is one volume; when one man dies, one chapter is not torn out of the book, but translated into a better language; and every chapter must be so translated; God employs several translators; some pieces are translated by age, some by sickness, some by war, some by justice; but God's hand is in every translation, and his hand shall bind up all our scattered leaves again, for that library where every book shall lie open to one another; as therefore the bell that rings to a sermon, calls not upon the preacher only, but upon the congregation to come; so this bell calls us all: but how much more me, who am brought so near the door by this sickness...

No man is an island, entire of itself; every man is a piece of the continent, a part of the main; if a clod be washed away by the sea, Europe is the less, as well as if a promontory were, as well as if a manor of thy friend's or of thine own were; any man's death diminishes me, because I am involved in mankind, and therefore never send to know for whom the bell tolls; it tolls for thee.

Before ordination into the Anglican Church in 1615 John Donne had seen the world and done it all. He had fought against the Spanish at Cadiz, seen his brother imprisoned in Newgate for harbouring a Catholic priest, his wife bear twelve children, and joined the diplomatic service. Such wide experience was grist to the mill of his poetry and prose. He was a love poet who wrote adventurously both about women and about God in a provocative and sometimes flirtatious style. Some of his opening lines are real show-stoppers:

'Busy old fool, unruly sun', he complains when morning interrupts his lovemaking.

'Batter my heart, three-personed God', he pleads with God when penitence proves elusive.

'Death be not proud.'

By the time *Devotions upon Emergent Occasions* was published, in which *Meditation 17* appears, Donne was Dean of St Paul's Cathedral with a wealth of life-experience behind him, which radiates through this mature reflection, his most famous passage of prose. Interconnectedness is the message: 'No man is an island'. Human beings are held together in a connectedness which is like the contiguity of a land mass: when a cliff is eroded and falls into the sea, the continent itself is diminished. This single image runs throughout the passage, making it like a poem, and indeed sometimes it is printed in short lines as if a kind of blank verse.

Donne's vision of connectedness provides a clear ethical critique of the contemporary world divided by terrorism, civil war, isolationism, protectionism, and an increasing poverty gap at a time of massive over-consumption. The key to Christianity's great theme of salvation is that God becomes human and therefore connected to every human being in the way John Donne describes, so that you might say Jesus of Nazareth's death 'diminishes me' because I am mortal like him. The theology of Christ's death is now most often understood of as God being crucified, and therefore as something God does for humankind (The Lamb of God who takes away the sin of the world), but here Donne's imagination suggests everyman partakes in it, an idea which fits St Paul's suggestion in Romans that in baptism one is buried with Christ and raised with him to new life. Connectedness therefore works, as it were, both vertically and horizontally – vertically with the divine and laterally between all human beings who, morally and for their own good, owe each other mutual respect and love.

Donne was one of the Metaphysical Poets, along with George Herbert, Andrew Marvell and others. His statue in St Paul's Cathedral is the only one to have survived, unscathed, from the Great Fire of 1666.

Digging Seamus Heaney (1939-2013)

Between my finger and my thumb
The squat pen rests; snug as a gun.

Under my window, a clean rasping sound
When the spade sinks into gravelly ground:
My father, digging. I look down

Till his straining rump among the flowerbeds
Bends low, comes up twenty years away
Stooping in rhythm through potato drills
Where he was digging.

The coarse boot nestled on the lug, the shaft
Against the inside knee was levered firmly.
He rooted out tall tops, buried the bright edge deep
To scatter new potatoes that we picked,
Loving their cool hardness in our hands.

By God, the old man could handle a spade.
Just like his old man.

My grandfather cut more turf in a day
Than any other man on Toner's bog.
Once I carried him milk in a bottle
Corked sloppily with paper. He straightened up
To drink it, then fell to right away
Nicking and slicing neatly, heaving sods
Over his shoulder, going down and down
For the good turf. Digging.

The cold smell of potato mould, the squelch and slap
Of soggy peat, the curt cuts of an edge
Through living roots awaken in my head.
But I've no spade to follow men like them.

Between my finger and my thumb
The squat pen rests.
I'll dig with it.

In this well-known poem, read by many at school, Irish poet Seamus Heaney describes how his father and his grandfather before him were experts at digging, and how their history, and in a sense Ireland's history, could be described in the metaphor of digging. The poet is less adept with a spade, but good with a pen as he points out in the opening lines:

'Between my finger and my thumb
The squat pen rests; as snug as a gun.'

The pen nestles into his hand as easily as the spade nestles to his father's body. The gun image suggests that the pen is mightier than the sword and that it might have been a better weapon in Ireland's sectarian history than the terrorist's gun. The closing lines of the poem are almost identical:

'Between my finger and my thumb
The squat pen rests.
I'll dig with it.'

Digging with a pen is, in a sense, absurd – far too small to dig the soil. So dig what? We can excavate history with a pen, grow new ideas with a pen, and a writer can do a day's work with a pen. But where does Good Friday come in? One might make the connection, although it would be a tenuous one, that the so-called 'Troubles' between Irish Protestants and Catholics, Ulster Unionists and Sinn Fein, with all the violence and terrorism over many decades that accompanied that conflict was significantly resolved in the Good Friday Agreement of Friday 10 April 1998 – but tenuous because this poem was published in 1966. Certainly the fact that the Agreement happened on a Good Friday resonated with anyone with a Christian sensibility, since on that day of all days when Christians believe Jesus 'takes away the sins of the world' it would seem a blasphemy to do violence to another person. In the Christian view of history the idea is that God (made man in Jesus Christ) suffers *with* humanity and his crucifixion by the Roman State embraces all human suffering, not least because crucifixion was a cruel punishment inflicted only on the alien and outsider, on offenders who were not Roman Citizens. This doesn't mean that God solves the problem of suffering – either why it happens or how its pain can be alleviated – but it does put suffering into a perspective which sees the universe, under God, as ultimately having meaning and purpose.

Okay, so none of this is in Heaney's poem, but the fact that through the contrasting images of a spade and a gun he so subtly links the simple pleasure of providing vegetables for the family table with the misery of the Troubles is enough for me to make the connection.

God's Grandeur Gerard Manley Hopkins (1844-1889)

The world is charged with the grandeur of God.
   It will flame out, like shining from shook foil;
   It gathers to a greatness, like the ooze of oil
Crushed. Why do men then now not reck his rod?
Generations have trod, have trod, have trod;
   And all is seared with trade; Bleared, smeared with toil;
   And wears man's smudge and shares man's smell: the soil
Is bare now, nor can foot feel, being shod.
And for all this, nature is never spent;
   There lives the dearest freshness deep down things;
And though the last lights off the black West went
   Oh, morning, at the brown brink eastward, springs —
Because the Holy Ghost over the bent
   World broods with warm breast and with ah! bright wings.

Talking about the previous poem I made the bold claim that the universe has meaning and purpose. Few philosophers would agree with this Christian interpretation. They'd more likely say the human mind, shaped by the experience of cause and effect, is tempted to read meaning into a physical order that is in every sense morally and intentionally neutral. It is us, when things go well, who have meaning and purpose, not the physical environment in which we live. You can't, for example, expect any compassion from nature.

But here is a Jesuit poet priest, Gerard Manley Hopkins, declaring, 'There lives the dearest freshness deep down things', a freshness which is the energy of the Holy Spirit, that third person of the Holy Trinity, always more mystifying to Christians than God the Creator or God the Son. Indeed the world is charged, like an electric current, with the grandeur of God and on occasions it flashes with epiphanies of light like the sun reflecting from metal foil or perhaps as the blinding light that Paul saw on the Road to Damascus.

Like Wordsworth in 'Tintern Abbey', Hopkins laments how the Industrial Revolution has despoiled nature with the grime of factories and cities. Maybe he was a dewy-eyed young romantic, a NIMBY on a grand scale. In 'Duns Scotus' Oxford' he says that in medieval Oxford 'country and town did / Once encounter in', but now it has 'a base and brickish skirt', referring to the suburban development of a part of North Oxford called Jericho. But he is passionate about the abuse of Nature as he sees it, 'all is seared with trade; Bleared, smeared with toil; / And wears man's smudge.' So in a more generous light one might see him as taking a stand against environmental degradation. Were he writing now he might rage against the melting of the icecaps and describe the irreversible crash of great chunks of ice falling away from the ice sheet into the sea. What it brings to the Good Friday vision is an assurance of God's underlying presence in creation, capable of redeeming corporate political greed as well as personal sin.

Although his poems were never published during his lifetime, his friend, the poet Robert Bridges, edited a volume of Hopkins's Poems that first appeared in 1918.

Thomas' sermon – *from* **Murder in the Cathedral** TS Eliot (1888-1965)

Reflect now, how Our Lord Himself spoke of Peace. He said to His disciples 'My peace I leave with you, my peace I give unto you.' Did He mean peace as we think of it: the kingdom of England at peace with its neighbours, the barons at peace with the King, the householder counting over his peaceful gains, the swept hearth, his best wine for a friend at the table, his wife singing to the children? Those men His disciples knew no such things: they went forth to journey afar, to suffer by land and sea, to know torture, imprisonment, disappointment, to suffer death by martyrdom. What then did He mean? If you ask that, remember then that He said also, 'Not as the world gives, give I unto you.' So then, He gave to His disciples peace, but not peace as the world gives.

Consider also one thing of which you have probably never thought. Not only do we at the feast of Christmas celebrate at once Our Lord›s Birth and His Death: but on the next day we celebrate the martyrdom of His first martyr, the blessed Stephen. Is it an accident, do you think, that the day of the first martyr follows immediately the day of the Birth of Christ? By no means. Just as we rejoice and mourn at once, in the Birth and in the Passion of Our Lord; so also, in a smaller figure, we both rejoice and mourn in the death of martyrs. We mourn, for the sins of the world that has martyred them; we rejoice, that another soul is numbered among the Saints in Heaven, for the glory of God and for the salvation of men...

A Christian martyrdom is never an accident, for Saints are not made by accident. Still less is a Christian martyrdom the effect of man's will to become a Saint, as a man by willing and contriving may become a ruler of men. A martyrdom is always the design of God, for His love of men, to warn them and to lead them, to bring them back to His ways. It is never the design of man; for the true martyr is he who has become the instrument of God, who has lost his will in the will of God, and who no longer desires anything for himself, not even the glory of becoming a martyr.

Playing Thomas in *Murder in the Cathedral* in 1962 was the highlight of my school acting career and 'preaching' this sermon helped persuade me becoming a priest might not be such a bad idea. Parents of other boys wrote in to the school to say they had been moved particularly by this part of the play, and as I spoke the words of the sermon I had been conscious of holding the audience in my grasp because, apart from the power of Eliot's words, I knew the text so well I was able to look the audience in the eye and speak them as if they were my own – a lesson any public speaker needs to learn.

The sermon is preached at the Christmas Morning Mass in Canterbury Cathedral and Eliot assumes the Archbishop could foresee his impending martyrdom, had felt it in his bones, and had time to reflect on what it meant. An important theme in the play is the temptation of seeking martyrdom for personal glory, choosing a path that would secure not only a place in heaven but fame for hundreds of years. You may think martyrdom unavoidable, something imposed on a person by an insecure State or paranoid Church. Once the courts, or the mob, are after you what chance have you got? But many martyrs can back out. Jesus needn't have gone to Jerusalem, he didn't have to turn over the tables of the money changers in the Temple, or take the lead after John the Baptist had been beheaded – warning enough. Thomas had the option to give in to the King but he stuck to his principles.

The juxtaposition of birth and death in the Christmas story, the key theme in the sermon, is picked up by many Christmas carols, most clearly in *The Holly and the Ivy* and the *Sans Day Carol*: 'Now the holly bears a berry as green as the grass, / And Mary bore Jesus, who died on the cross.' And also in carols about the Wise Men, whose gifts of gold, frankincense, and myrrh make the same point, myrrh signifying the preparation of Jesus' body for burial. Did Mary know Jesus' destiny? The idea of destiny is more complex than simple cause and effect, as in: it was written in the stars that Derek would become a great tennis player. When we speak of destiny we usually do so retrospectively, recognising how the events of a life, or a life so far, have coalesced to push a person in a particular direction. In *The Noise of Time* Julian Barnes says, 'destiny was only the words *And so.*' I might add *Things happen*. The word derives from the Latin verb *destinare*, to establish or make firm, so when we speak on fulfilling one's destiny, it's about living up to your potential and building on the foundation of your past.

The Corpus Christi Carol

Lully, lullay, lully, lullay,
The falcon hath borne my make away.

He bore him up, he bore him down,
He bore him in to an orchard brown.

And in that orchard there was a hall,
And it was hanged with purple and pall.

In that hall there was a bed
It was hanged with gold so red.

In that bed there lieth a knight,
His woundės bleeding day and night.

By that bed's side there kneeleth a may,
And she weepeth both night and day.

And by that bed's side there standeth a stone,
'Corpus Christi' written thereon.

I have hesitated about the inclusion of this most evocative of carols because it's not at all clear that it refers in any way to Christ's Passion. Even the opening line, so gently picturing a mother rocking her baby to sleep, seems to be borrowed from elsewhere and bears little relation to what follows. The text here is the one provided by Helen Gardner in the *Faber Book of Religious Verse*, which she says is the original sixteenth-century version, connected with the Abbey at Glastonbury. It is of course possible to interpret the knight as Christ and the 'may' or maiden as the Virgin Mary weeping for her son and the stone inscribed 'Corpus Christi' as signifying the Holy Eucharist. Indeed there is some suggestion that this poem is associated with the Arthurian legend of the Holy Grail, the cup of the Last Supper said to have been brought to Britain by Joseph of Arimathea, but lost for centuries. The great unifying objective of the Knights of the Round Table was to find the chalice, supposedly kept in a castle surrounded by a wasteland and guarded by a custodian called the Fisher King, who suffered from a wound that would never heal until the cup was claimed.

A further suggestion, largely rejected, is that since the falcon was the heraldic symbol on the arms of Anne Boleyn's family, this could be a poem sympathetic to the suffering of Katharine of Aragon, the first wife of Henry VIII, who in her exile from court maintained an almost monastic discipline of devotion and prayer, frequently receiving the bread of the mass, the body of Christ, in Latin 'Corpus Christi'.

Nevertheless, I have included it because when I read the carol, without trying to unscramble the words or treat it as a sort of 'Da Vinci Code', I find the imagery so enigmatic and prolific.

This bread I break Dylan Thomas (1914-1953)

This bread I break was once the oat,
This wine upon a foreign tree
Plunged in its fruit;
Man in the day or wine at night
Laid the crops low, broke the grape's joy.

Once in this time wine the summer blood
Knocked in the flesh that decked the vine,
Once in this bread
The oat was merry in the wind;
Man broke the sun, pulled the wind down.

This flesh you break, this blood you let
Make desolation in the vein,
Were oat and grape
Born of the sensual root and sap;
My wine you drink, my bread you snap.

In *Under Milk Wood* Dylan Thomas paints a picture of religion in his town: 'in the chill, squat chapel, hymning in bonnet and brooch and bombazine black, butterfly choker and bootlace bow, coughing like nannygoats, suckling mintoes, fortywinking hallelujah.' It's a mocking portrayal but reveals roots reaching deep into a Christian culture. 'Starless and bible-black' is how he describes the night in the first line of the same play.

He was a rebel who despite his intellectual ability dropped out of school at sixteen to become a junior reporter for the *South Wales Daily Post*. Seven years later he met a dancer, in a pub in London, Caitlin Macnamara, who at the time was Augustus John's mistress. They had an affair and married, but despite their passion for each other, both struggled to be faithful.

So Thomas was both a reckless and a sensual man, in love with the sensuality of language and taken with its potential for alliterative, generative excitement. You find it to a smaller degree in this interpretation of the Last Supper where he celebrates the natural exuberance of growth in the cornfield and summer vineyard. The wild, uninhibited freedom of juice and grain is tamed and constrained into the bread and wine on the table. In the second stanza the vitality of the 'summer blood' in the grape reminds him of sexual intercourse, which he evokes with the crude slang word 'knocked', suggesting as it does an easy, casual relationship. And two lines later, the idea of the oat being 'merry' hints at intoxication and good company. It is man, both in his sinfulness and his Welsh-chapel puritanism, who breaks the sun and the grape's joy and who pulls the wind down and lays the crops low. In some sense Christ's ministry is 'born of the sensual root and sap' in its uninhibited freedom and radical ethics, from eating and drinking with tax collectors and sinners, the embrace of the unclean leper, to the injunction to love your enemy and do good to those that hate you. People miss this prolific *joie de vivre* and readiness to break the conventional code thus draining Christ's bread and wine of its sap and turning it into an organised religion.

So Thomas sets the cat amongst the pigeons by weaving

sexual imagery into his picture of the crucifixion. What should be the response? Shouts of, 'Blasphemy'? The burning of books? The anathematisation of Dylan Thomas? No, this poem proclaims nature's prolific innocence. Redemption is about life, and life is about the material and the sensual and the moral frailty of human beings. Redemption means nothing when there is nothing to be redeemed.

Triptych Andrew Motion (born 1952)

1. In the Wilderness

What does a man see
in the wilderness
if not a reed shaken by the wind?

Since I arrived here
I have admired thousands
for the music they produce –

astringent in summer,
in winter fuller and nearly sweet
thanks to the green moisture in the leaf.

As for human visitors
and their wish to get in touch,
there has only been this stranger,
who if he spoke at all
argued with his shadow.

So far as I can tell
nothing altered when he went.

I still bathe myself in streams
poured out by the desert lark;

I read the news I need
in the footprints of lizards

and the looping hieroglyphics
snakes leaves with their skin.

2. Lazarus

I slipped over the border.

I fell down into the pure dark
with no dreaming.

Then I came home again.

Wherever I go now –
to market in the village,
or brushing through the fields at harvest –
I like to imagine
I leave swirling trails of light.

In truth there is nothing so obvious
to show me unlike
the man I was before.

And yet to speak in confidence
I am almost worn through
by the terms of my existence.

They require me to raise my voice
every single day
and declare that I am happy.

3. The Upper Room

My task is to clear the room
when the guests go home at night.

To straighten the benches,

to sweep up the bread-crumbs,
fish skeletons and stalks of peppers,

to separate the olives from the olive stones,

and lastly to wipe away the stain
if any wine has spilt between the pitcher and the cups.

This triptych of poems (like a three-panelled painting behind an altar) was read by the author, before it was published, in a sermon preached at the University Church in Oxford. The following Good Friday we included it in our readings. At the beginning of his address, Andrew Motion explained the basis on which he had accepted the invitation to speak in church: 'I am one of thousands, millions I dare say, who have a great appetite for faith and a great curiosity about its nature, and a great love for the Church of England (despite all the things that also drive me mad about it), but who struggles to sign up to the articles of faith that are spelt out in the Creed. Who struggles, but who nevertheless hears the word of God continuing to speak, in ways that are sometimes clear, but often parallel, subterranean, partial, muffled, on the edge of hearing.'

'In the Wilderness' begins with the image of a 'reed shaken by the wind', which makes a kind of music as the wind blows through it. In the gospels it's a symbol of weakness. Jesus says to the crowds: When you went into the wilderness to listen to John the Baptist, you didn't go to hear a reed shaken by the wind but a radical prophet in rough clothing. In the poem Andrew Motion creates with it an atmosphere of loneliness and isolation where Jesus spent time arguing 'with his shadow', a beautifully poetic way of describing how at the beginning of his ministry Jesus spent a long time by himself working out his priorities, deciding who he was, and convincing himself that God had a uniquely important mission for him.

In the second panel of the triptych we meet Lazarus, raised from the dead by Jesus in one of the most pivotal miraculous signs related in St John's Gospel. Unsurprisingly Lazarus becomes so famous he imagines he shines with celestial light even when out shopping, but he's no different from what he was before the miracle, except that now he finds it hard to be happy in the way everyone expects him to be. The New Testament doesn't tell us how Lazarus felt about his astonishing experience or what it was like to be a superstar of the new messianic age, but Motion has put his finger on a basic truth, that religion is no panacea for the ills of the world and it's a mistake ever to think that somehow after a major religious experience, even a miracle as comprehensive as being raised from the dead, nothing will ever go wrong again.

If this is true at a personal level it's also true at the political level: the messianic age Jesus is said to usher in cannot be an age of perfect politics or a world where the need for politics is over. Resurrection, or Easter Joy as it is proclaimed two days after Good Friday, doesn't mean immunity from sadness, depression, violence or tragedy, for example, although it may mean one is better equipped to face those challenges.

In the third panel we are listening to the servant who waits table in the Upper Room Restaurant. Rather cleverly Andrew Motion reflects on the passion through events that happen before the crucifixion, but each of which are important to it: in the wilderness, Jesus determines the course his life is going to take; the Raising of Lazarus prefigures Jesus' own resurrection; and at the Last Supper in the upper room Jesus says of the bread and wine, this is my body and this is my blood. The upper room waiter doesn't mention this, but he does speak of wiping away the stain of spilt wine, which makes one think of bloodstains and possibly of Judas' betrayal of Jesus, but also the idea that Jesus' blood might wipe away the stain of human sin or wrongdoing. The poem is sparse, like a Terry Frost print or a Matisse paper cut-out, so that this particular triptych provides the essence of a picture, its linear motifs and fundamental colours, rather than a luxuriant Old Master painting.

from **Psalm 22**

MY God, my God, look upon me; why hast thou forsaken
me: and art so far from my health, and from the words of my
complaint?
2 O my God, I cry in the day-time, but thou hearest not : and in
the night-season also I take no rest.
3 And thou continuest holy : O thou worship of Israel.
4 Our fathers hoped in thee : they trusted in thee, and thou
didst deliver them.
5 They called upon thee, and were holpen : they put their trust
in thee, and were not confounded.
6 But as for me, I am a worm, and no man : a very scorn of men,
and the outcast of the people.
7 All they that see me laugh me to scorn : they shoot out their
lips, and shake their heads, saying,
8 He trusted in God, that he would deliver him : let him deliver
him, if he will have him.
14 I am poured out like water, and all my bones are out of joint:
my heart also in the midst of my body is even like melting wax.
15 My strength is dried up like a potsherd, and my tongue
cleaveth to my gums : and thou shalt bring me into the dust of
death.
16 For many dogs are come about me : and the council of the
wicked layeth siege against me.
17 They pierced my hands and my feet; I may tell all my bones :
they stand staring and looking upon me.
18 They part my garments among them : and cast lots upon my
vesture.
19 But be not thou far from me, O Lord : thou art my succour,
haste thee to help me.
20 Deliver my soul from the sword : my darling from the power
of the dog.
21 Save me from the lion's mouth : thou hast heard me also
from among the horns of the unicorns.

Poetry doesn't easily make the transition from one language to another, but the Psalms are an exception. They've travelled from Hebrew, through Greek and Latin, to the wonderfully creative English of the sixteenth century. In the hands of Myles Coverdale, around 1535, they took the shape familiar to anyone who has attended choral evensong in their cathedral or parish church. Coverdale's is the version used in the Book of Common Prayer. The principal writer of the English Prayer Book, Thomas Cranmer, was brilliant at prose but not so hot on poetry, so Coverdale's psalms were incorporated from the Great Bible of 1539. In his prose writing Cranmer finds a resonant rhythm by using Latin and Anglo Saxon words in parallel, as for example in the collect for Ash Wednesday: 'Create and make in us new and contrite hearts', rather than the much plainer alternative: make our hearts contrite. In the Psalms there is a similar poetic rhythm achieved by repetition or parallel opposites as in verse two of Psalm 22 where day and night stand in contrast: 'O my God, I cry in the day-time, but thou hearest not : and in the night-season also I take no rest.' What gives the psalms an added piquancy is their readiness to protest to God, their bold anger with God for human misery and suffering: 'O my God, I cry in the day-time, but thou hearest not.' Damn you.

For me the most awe-inspiring moment in the Good Friday liturgy has always been the austere singing of this psalm in the minor key to Anglican Chant, evoking a recollection of the depth of human suffering: 'all my bones are out of joint' and 'my tongue cleaveth to my gums'. I imagine the tortured victim screaming in pain from broken or dislocated bones, mouth parched with thirst and fear. No wonder this text was part of the undergirding structure for the gospel narrative of the crucifixion of Jesus. The familiar quotations punctuate the psalm as it is sung: 'My God, my God… why hast thou forsaken me; he trusted in God, let him deliver him; they pierced my hands and my feet, they cast lots for my vesture.' At the time it was written crucifixion was unknown in the Hebrew experience, but so closely has the psalm become associated with the cross in the Christian tradition that some translators have been tempted to tweak the words even more in their own direction and many scholars argue that a better rendition of 'they pierced my hands and my feet' would be 'like a lion, they are at my hands and feet'. This of course would make it seem much less like a prophecy of the crucifixion.

The Moon in Lleyn RS Thomas (1913-2000)

The last quarter of the moon
of Jesus gives way
to the dark; the serpent
digests the egg. Here
on my knees in this stone
church, that is full only
of the silent congregation
of shadows and the sea's
sound, it is easy to believe
Yeats was right. Just as though
choirs had not sung, shells
have swallowed them; the tide laps
at the Bible; the bell fetches
no people to the brittle miracle
of bread. The sand is waiting
for the running back of the grains
in the wall into its blond
glass. Religion is over, and
what will emerge from the body
of the new moon, no one
can say.

But a voice sounds
in my ear. Why so fast,
mortal? These very seas
are baptized. The parish
has a saint's name time cannot
unfrock. In cities that
have outgrown their promise people
are becoming pilgrims
again, if not to this place,
then to the recreation of it
in their own spirits. You must remain
kneeling. Even as this moon

making its way through the earth's
cumbersome shadow, prayer, too,
has its phases.

There are echoes here of what we read in Carol Ann Duffy's 'Some days, although we cannot pray, a prayer / utters itself...' Duffy finds a kind of religious epiphany in the sound of a train, a child playing the piano, and the early morning shipping forecast. Here R.S. Thomas uses Yeats' famous image of faith receding like the tide going out over Dover Beach: 'Religion is over.'

'...the tide laps
at the Bible; the bell fetches
no people to the brittle miracle
of bread.'

But, he says, 'A voice sounds in my ear... prayer too has its phases', like the moon. Despite doubt and the questioning of faith, he has a nagging feeling that there's something in it that must be respected, not recklessly abandoned. It's religious instinct, I think, rather than hard to shake off cultural conditioning. Philip Larkin reached a similar conclusion in his poem, 'Church Going', in which he describes visiting a little-used church where he mocks the religion it used to represent, but to his surprise discovers 'a hunger in himself to be more serious' – that shock of the numinous, which Soren Kierkegaard explores in his classic 'Fear and trembling'.

This doubt might seem a modern dilemma, but it's ancient as the Bible itself, as we have seen in Psalm 22 and its quotation by Jesus from the cross in Mark and Matthew's gospels: 'My God, My God, why have you forsaken me?'

Here doubt is placed at the centre of Christian theology, at the very point in the story where salvation is achieved in the death of Christ, acknowledging the underlying experience of the silence of God and how, in the deepest hour of need, however hard you pray, God might not answer. It has always seemed to me doubt is the flip side of faith – a natural, inevitable, and proper part of it. Some people say this is merely to surrender Christianity to the spirit of the age. But that is to miss the point. It is optimising faith, not minimising it. In fact, the Church would be wise and honest to admit the difficulties of faith in the present secular age, and to give permission to its members to express their misgivings and to include all seekers, doubters, questioners, and confused persons who wish to be part of the Body of Christ. There really can't be any point excluding people who are searching for God, and generally inclined to support the Church, however uncommittedly, just because they don't believe in exactly the same way as traditional doctrine suggests they ought.

Love III George Herbert (1593-1633)

Love bade me welcome. Yet my soul drew back
    Guilty of dust and sin.
But quick-eyed Love, observing me grow slack
    From my first entrance in,
Drew nearer to me, sweetly questioning,
    If I lacked any thing.

A guest, I answered, worthy to be here:
    Love said, You shall be he.
I the unkind, ungrateful? Ah my dear,
    I cannot look on thee.
Love took my hand, and smiling did reply,
    Who made the eyes but I?

Truth Lord, but I have marred them: let my shame
    Go where it doth deserve.
And know you not, says Love, who bore the blame?
    My dear, then I will serve.
You must sit down, says Love, and taste my meat:
    So I did sit and eat.

Born in 1593, in the reign of Elizabeth I, into an aristocratic Welsh family, Herbert was educated at Trinity College, Cambridge and spent the first part of his career in the University as Public Orator. He died just forty years later as a modest country parson in the parish of Bemerton, within walking distance of Salisbury Cathedral. The devotional poetry he wrote throughout his short life is considered the best of its kind in English literature.

In this poem Love is capitalised to indicate Christ or God. The writer of the First Epistle of John declares, 'God is love, and those who abide in love abide in God, and God abides in them.' (1 John 4.16). Here the scene is a great banquet, such as we find in the New Testament in, for example, the story of the Great Banquet when the smart invited guests make their excuses and the servants are instructed to invite everyone in from the streets (Matthew 22.1-9). Such stories are considered to be variations on the theme of the Last Supper. Herbert probably had this in mind when he wrote the line, 'You must sit down, says Love, and taste my meat.' This is my body given for you. But he combines the image with a picture of the kind of feast given by a land owner to his tenants and farm labourers at harvest or mid-winter. For the guest it's like going into a room full of people you don't know and coming over all shy. Like a good host, 'Quick-eyed Love' is alert to the self-conscious guest standing alone and immediately tries to put her at her ease. In fact the guest is not easily to be reassured and protests her unworthiness to be present there in the company of one so great and all-seeing. It is one of the essential characteristics of love to see the quality of the other and not to be blinded by one's own selfishness. And that is what this poem declares loud and clear to me. When the self-effacing guest says, 'Let my shame/go where it doth deserve' – presumably to hell or to some kind of punishment – Love claims to be he 'who bore the blame'. In other words, the one who redeems the sinner. And there we are brought back to the cross and to Good Friday in the sense that Christians always understand the central act of salvation and forgiveness to be Christ's sacrificial death. Other aspects of his self-giving love, evident for example in his willingness to embrace the leper, go the extra mile, and welcome women into his inner circle, contribute to salvation, but the crucifixion is the central act. This was a view held by Irenaeus in the Second Century that the whole of Christ's life brought salvation or newness of life, not just the moment of his death.

Preached before the King's Majesty, at Whitehall, on the Sixth of April, A.D. 1604, being Good Friday Lancelot Andrewes (1555-1626)

Text Lamentations 1:12
'Is it nothing to you, all ye that pass by? Behold, and see if there be any sorrow like unto My sorrow, which is done unto Me, wherewith the Lord hath afflicted Me in the day of His fierce anger.

Consider then the inestimable benefit that groweth unto you from this incomparable love. It is not impertinent this, even this, that to us hereby all is turned about clean contrary; that 'by His stripes we are healed,' by His sweat we refreshed, by His forsaking we received to grace. That this day, to Him the day of the fierceness of God's wrath, is to us the day of the fulness of God's favour, as the Apostle calleth it, 'a day of salvation.' In respect of that He suffered, I deny not, an evil day, a day of heaviness; but in respect of that which He by it hath obtained for us, it is as we truly call it a good day, a day of joy and jubilee. For it doth not only rid us of that wrath which pertaineth to us for our sins; but farther, it maketh that pertain to us whereto we had no manner of right at all.

For not only by His death as death by the death of our sacrifice, by the blood of His cross as by the blood of the paschal lamb, the destroyer passeth over us, and we shall not perish; but also by His death, as by the death of our High Priest for He is Priest and Sacrifice both we restored from our exile, even to our former forfeited estate in the land of Promise. Or rather, as the Apostle saith, *non sicut delictum sic donum*; not to the same estate, but to one nothing like it, that is, one far better than the estate our sins bereft us. For they deprived us of Paradise, a place on earth; but by the purchase of His blood we are entitled to a far higher, even the Kingdom of Heaven; and His blood, not only the blood of 'remission,' to acquit us of our sins, but 'the blood of the Testament too,' to bequeath us and give us estate in that Heavenly inheritance.'

Lancelot Andrewes distinguished himself as a clergyman in the reign of Elizabeth I, but rose to great favour under James I who enjoyed his preaching both for its content and its style, made him a bishop and gave him prominence in the preparation of the King James Bible, often known as the *Authorized Version*. When this sermon was preached in Whitehall Palace, James had been on throne but one year, Shakespeare was writing *Measure for Measure,* and the publication of the King James Bible lay seven years hence.

If we make the effort to see across the gulf in language and literary form which separates late medieval England from the twenty-first century, it's hard to miss the oratorical power of this preacher who begins by raising our sympathy for the victim on the cross – 'Is it nothing to you all ye that pass by?' You are healed by his stripes and by his sweat refreshed. On the one hand we see the 'fierceness of God's wrath' imposed on Jesus, on the other the massive benefit offered by God in return – complete relief from God's wrath and a salvation 'we had no manner of right [to] at all.' That's why the day is called 'Good' Friday.

In the next paragraph he develops the imagery of blood – the lamb's blood daubed by the Israelites on their door posts as a sign to the angel of death to pass over their houses when God punished the Egyptians by killing their first born, and the blood spilled by the High Priest in Jerusalem on the Day of Atonement. The feast of the Atonement is the one day in the year when the High Priest was permitted to enter the Holy of Holies to make sacrifice, and in the Epistle to the Hebrews Christ is described as the 'Great High Priest' who enters heaven as both priest and victim sacrificing himself for the sins of the world, setting humans and God 'at one' for all time. Andrewes is a Protestant, drawing from the tradition of the French Reformer, John Calvin, and cementing the English Reformation which had undergone a stuttering settling-down period in the reign of Elizabeth. In the last sentence of the extract, he speaks of the remission of sins and also the 'blood of the Testament' which refers not to the biblical New Testament, but to the new covenant, or new deal, between God and humans which guarantees what Andrewes calls a 'heavenly inheritance'.

Whereas poetry tends to pose questions, this jam-packed prose sets out to develop and justify an argument and therefore seems to require more commentary. I find the idea of 'God's wrath', with all the subsequent emphasis on blood sacrifice, worrying because I see in it the potential for a violent theology that endorses punitive behaviour. Is salvation best expressed in these terms? Couldn't an all-powerful God simply issue an edict declaring salvation a done deal? Isn't it unfortunate for contemporary Christianity that this important notion of redemption is trapped in the language and imagery of animal sacrifice, which we now find so culturally alien, despite the cruelty undoubtedly perpetrated in intensive animal farming in Britain? And doesn't the elevation of a wrathful God empower those who think corporal punishment and violence within relationship is acceptable and even a good thing? But Andrewes is heading down this road in the nicest possible way, without any thought of justifying violence as he endorses the theory of atonement known as *penal substitution*. In summary, penal substitution argues that a punitive God requires justice for human sin and decides his own son will take the punishment on behalf of humankind by suffering crucifixion.

The standard defence given by those who hold the theory of Substitutionary Atonement is that God is good because he refuses to impose this cruelty on someone else, he imposes it on himself because he is wholly present in Christ. Whether you buy into this interpretation is up to you, but it looks suspect to me.

The Merchant of Venice **Act 4 Scene 1** William Shakespeare (1564-1616)

The quality of mercy is not strain'd.
It droppeth as the gentle rain from heaven
Upon the place beneath. It is twice blest:
It blesseth him that gives, and him that takes.
'Tis mightiest in the mightiest; it becomes
The throned monarch better than his crown.
His scepter shows the force of temporal power,
The attribute to awe and majesty,
Wherein doth sit the dread and fear of kings;
But mercy is above this sceptered sway;
It is enthroned in the heart of kings;
It is an attribute to God himself;
And earthly power doth then show likest God's
When mercy seasons justice.

Portia's famous speech, as counsel for the defence representing Antonio against Shylock, in the *Merchant of Venice* offers a gloss on the previous passage. Antonio had failed to repay Shylock a sum of money he'd borrowed on the surety of a pound of his own flesh, and Shylock demands his compensation insisting it be taken from Antonio's heart. Blood and justice are again involved, but not quite as one expects. As the trial continues Portia adopts the tactic that of course Shylock must have justice, but the bond allows only for flesh and not blood to be taken. If a drop of blood is spilled then Shylock will forfeit everything. In a way, I prefer to take this speech out of context, because the ultimate insult visited upon Shylock is that he must convert to Christianity and, to the modern mind, the play descends into a racist, anti-Semitic diatribe. But at face value these words encapsulate the essence of divine mercy, which blesses both those who show it and those who receive it and, being a more important symbol of kingship than the crown, provides the template for the moral exercise of political power. In fact it's an attribute of God and when 'mercy seasons justice' then people act like God – rather different from 'God's wrath' and the slaughter of sacrificial animals. In fact, one might see the character of substitutionary atonement more in the behaviour of Shylock, and maybe this was in the back of Shakespeare's mind.

Tomorrow, and tomorrow, and tomorrow (from *Macbeth*;
spoken by Macbeth)
William Shakespeare (1564-1616) (first performed 1606)

Tomorrow, and tomorrow, and tomorrow,
Creeps in this petty pace from day to day,
To the last syllable of recorded time;
And all our yesterdays have lighted fools
The way to dusty death. Out, out, brief candle!
Life's but a walking shadow, a poor player,
That struts and frets his hour upon the stage,
And then is heard no more. It is a tale
Told by an idiot, full of sound and fury,
Signifying nothing.

In order to do its work theology needs raw material, the raw material of experience. Redemption is all very well as a pious ideal, but we need to know what is to be redeemed. In this bleak and dystopian rant at the meaninglessness of being, from a tyrant whose ruthless power-grab has left him knee-deep in murderous blood, Shakespeare sets out the most fundamental agenda for salvation: to find meaning and purpose in a seemingly uncaring universe.

Shakespeare trawls his own experience as an actor for an image of futility. In *As You Like It*, Act II, Scene VII he says:

All the world's a stage
And all the men and women merely players;
They have their exits and their entrances...
[the] Last scene of all,
That ends this strange eventful history,
Is second childishness and mere oblivion,
Sans teeth, sans eyes, sans taste, sans everything.

Good Friday, 1613. Riding Westward John Donne (1572-1631)

Let man's Soule be a Sphere, and then, in this,
The intelligence that moves, devotion is,
And as the other Spheres, by being grown
Subject to foreign motion, lose their own,
And being by others hurried every day,
Scarce in a year their natural form obey:
Pleasure or business, so, our Soules admit
For their first mover, and are whirled by it.
Hence is't, that I am carried towards the West
This day, when my Soules form bends toward the East.
There I should see a Sun, by rising set,
And by that setting endless day beget;
But that Christ on this Crosse, did rise and fall,
Sin had eternally benighted all.
Yet dare I almost be glad, I do not see
That spectacle of too much weight for me.
Who sees Gods face, that is self life, must die;
What a death were it then to see God die?
It made his own Lieutenant Nature shrink,
It made his footstool crack, and the Sun wink.
Could I behold those hands which span the Poles,
And tune all spheres at once pierced with those holes?
Could I behold that endless height which is
Zenith to us, and our Antipodes,
Humbled below us? or that blood which is
The seat of all our Souls, if not of his,
Made dirt of dust, or that flesh which was worn
By God, for his apparel, ragg'd, and torn?
If on these things I durst not look, durst I
Upon his miserable mother cast mine eye,
Who was Gods partner here, and furnished thus
Half of that Sacrifice, which ransomed us?
Though these things, as I ride, be from mine eye,

They are present yet unto my memory,
For that looks towards them; and thou look'st towards me,
O Saviour, as thou hang'st upon the tree;
I turn my back to thee, but to receive
Corrections, till thy mercies bid thee leave.
O think me worth thine anger, punish me,
Burn off my rusts, and my deformity,
Restore thine Image, so much, by thy grace,
That thou may'st know me, and I'll turn my face.

Teenage verse speakers aside, anyone might be grateful for a bit of unpacking here. The clue is in the title, 'riding westward'. The events of Good Friday took place in what to us in Europe is the 'Middle East'. Presumably on that particular day in 1613 John Donne had urgent business pressing him to set out from Warwickshire to Wales, and as the evening sun got in his eyes he didn't miss the irony of it: he had turned his back on the thing that was most important to him, the Passion of Christ, and was travelling in the opposite direction. As he rides, with the rhythm of the poem possibly mimicking the stride of his horse, he expands the image.

The poem begins with the complex imagery of celestial spheres – the sun, the planets, the soul as a sphere, and perhaps even the idea of his head, albeit only the size of a football, as a kind of sphere turned by the gravitational pull of the sun, on this occasion to the west. When the poem was written Galileo was developing the Copernican theory of heliocentricity, so it was high in the intellectual agenda of the day. As planets orbit the sun, Donne thought, so the soul as a sphere should orbit the Son. He wants Christocentricity – everything to revolve about Christ.

The key to the poem is in this play on words between the sun – which rises in the east – and the Son (of God) who also, as it were, rises in the east at the resurrection. As the poet heads westwards, away from the crucifixion, he is looking towards the setting sun and the night that will follow it and he thinks to himself, even if I were to turn back towards the light of Jesus, on this day I would only see darkness, the dreadful sight of his tortured body and, of course, the solar eclipse which Matthew describes in chapter 27.45 of his gospel, 'From noon on, darkness came over the whole land until three in the afternoon.' Yet for all that, if Christ hadn't suffered, Donne suggests, sin would have cast everyone into eternal darkness:

'But that Christ on this Crosse, did rise and fall,
(like the sun)
Sinne had eternally benighted all.'

He is glad not to have to look on these terrible events, and excuses himself to some degree with the thought, 'Who sees Gods face, that is selfe life, must die' – a reference to Exodus 33.20 where God says to Moses, 'for no one shall see me and live.' But Donne also feels unworthy to look on God and concludes the poem with the hope that through penitence he may be sufficiently cleansed – 'burn off my rusts and my deformity' – to turn around and behold God.

If a little inaccessible, the language isn't difficult, and when you dig beneath it the East-West paradox comes to the surface as a compelling take on the Christian dilemma of discipleship.

Pontius Pilate discusses the Proceedings of the Last Judgement Vassar Miller (1924-1998)

Unfortunate. Yet how was I to know,
Appointed to preserve the Pax Romana,
that he was not another of these fools
whose crosses bristled on the hills like toothpicks.
And how were you to guess that the young girl
you burned one day in France for hearing Voices
was destined to be hailed as saint and genius,
not merely silly in the head from sex?
Most of her kind would be. And it's the duty
of men like us to save the world from madness.
Never mind who saves the world from sin.
For madness does the harm that we can see,
strangles the baby, sets the house on fire,
and rapes the women in the name of powers
we can't, nine times out of ten. And if
we are wrong the tenth time, why should we be blamed?
That judge, now, over there, he'll sit in honor
simply because he happened to follow the way
his nose led him to declare the fellow
who knelt barefooted at the Communion Rail
in a suburban church a poor crazy
son-of-a-bitch. He bet on a sure thing
and won. Our gambles look the same. We lost.
He really and truly was the Son of God?
I'm not surprised. The gods will play some joke –
and then get angry every time it works.

Vassar Miller was born in Houston, Texas where she lived all her life, confined by a lifelong struggle with cerebral palsy which made even the simplest tasks burdensome. In 1961 she was shortlisted for the Pulitzer Prize for her collection of poems, *Wage War on Silence*. A Houston Chronicle reviewer wrote in 1991, 'Her subjects are the same ones that keep most people searching beyond and beneath the surfaces of their daily lives; love, life, emotions and the unfilled longings of the disabled.' She was a devout Christian who often explored religious themes in a forthright way, as she does in this poem, where Pilate excuses his own lack of judgement by suggesting that it's good enough for judges to get it right nine times out of ten. Besides, they were mistaken over Joan of Arc. But they get it right with the easy targets, where perhaps nobody cares: the homeless and malodorous and crazy characters who cause disruption when they enter churches in search of tenderness and a couple of quid.

I never forget the redemptive story, told me by a colleague, of the homeless man who came to the foot washing ceremony on Maundy Thursday when, following Jesus' example with his disciples, the clergy wash the feet of selected parishioners. The custom is that each person offers only one foot for washing. This guy was one of those selected and after he had peeled off his sock and had his smelly foot thoroughly washed he said, 'Ah, that was lovely. Now can you do the other one?' Of course my friend obliged.

Collect for Ash Wednesday

Almighty and everlasting God,
who hatest nothing that thou hast made
and dost forgive the sins of all them that are penitent:
create and make in us new and contrite hearts
that we, worthily lamenting our sins
and acknowledging our wretchedness,
may obtain of thee, the God of all mercy,
perfect remission and forgiveness;
through Jesus Christ thy Son our Lord.
Amen.

Prayer of St Francis of Assisi

Lord, make me an instrument of your peace;
where there is hatred, let me sow love;
where there is injury, pardon:
where there is doubt, faith ;
where there is despair, hope
where there is darkness, light
where there is sadness, joy
O divine Master,
grant that I may not so much seek to be consoled as to console;
to be understood, as to understand;
to be loved, as to love;
for it is in giving that we receive,
it is in pardoning that we are pardoned,
and it is in dying that we are born to Eternal Life.
Amen.

Collect for the Sunday next before Easter

Almighty and everlasting God,
who of thy tender love towards mankind
hast sent thy Son our Saviour Jesus Christ
to take upon him our flesh
and to suffer death upon the cross:
grant that we may follow the example of his patience and
humility,
and also be made partakers of his resurrection;
through Jesus Christ thy Son our Lord.
Amen.

Prayer of St Teresa of Avila

Christ has no body now on earth but yours,
No hands, no feet but yours.
Yours are the eyes through which the compassion of Christ
Looks out upon the world;
Yours the feet with which he goes about doing good.
Yours are the hands with which Christ blesses the world.
Christ has no body now on earth but yours.

Prayer of St. Richard of Chichester (1197-1253)

Thanks be to thee my Lord Jesus Christ
For all the benefits thou hast won for me,
For all the pains and insults thou hast borne for me.

O most merciful Redeemer, Friend, and Brother,
May I know thee more clearly,
Love thee more dearly,
And follow thee more nearly
Day by day.
Amen.

Are prayers poems? Sometimes, especially more formal ones using colourful imagery to make their point. Take for example Cranmer's collect for the Seventh Sunday after Trinity:

'Lord of all power and might, who art the author and giver of all good things: *Graft* in our hearts the love of thy name, *increase* in us true religion, *nourish* us with all goodness, and of thy great mercy keep us in the same; through Jesus Christ our Lord. Amen.'

Here the image of grafting paints a picture of a gardener cutting a shoot from one tree and splicing it into the rootstock of another, as is still done today when propagating most fruit trees. So the prayer asks for the love for God to be grafted into the rootstock of the petitioner's heart. The gardening theme continues with 'increase', the same root word as 'crescent' as in a growing moon, or 'crescendo' in music. The grafted shoot is to grow and blossom, nourished – fed and watered – by goodness. On the other hand the Prayer of St Teresa of Avila is not like a prayer at all, more like a statement. Who is the speaker of this prayer? God, the Church, or maybe one's conscience? It's like an admonition to live a life of discipleship following in the footsteps of Christ.

Informal prayer tends to be more chatty, more prosaic, and therefore fleeting, although nonetheless valid because of it. Most people think prayer is primarily about asking for things, petitionary prayer, but for some it is can be silence, contemplation, waiting, tuning in. The idea of tuning in appeals to me. In 'The Brain: the story of you' David Engleman, discussing the way in which human brains operate with one another in a rich web of interaction, explains how when we see someone else being hurt part of our own pain matrix becomes activated and we feel emotional empathy. I hope some of the pieces in this book spark the pain matrix as they contemplate Jesus' crucifixion, and that art and the triumphalist theology of Christ's victory over death hasn't so distanced the historical reality that such evolutionary empathy is rubbed out. Similarly, in prayer, the interrelatedness of human brains is further enriched by the idea of being linkedin and networked with what you might call the divine mind, the mysterious reality of God.

The few prayers chosen here have a durability accrued by much use and repetition, familiar friends capable of creating a prayerful disposition or summing up intentions that are otherwise difficult to put into words. That's why some are called 'collects', because they collect together the thoughts of the person praying and often enable a prayer that otherwise couldn't be spoken, in a not dissimilar way from what Carol Ann Duffy found in her poem, 'Prayer'. So in this sense prayers can be like poems: they cause you to think or see in a way that you hadn't before and increase, as it were, the spiritual vocabulary.

Copyright Acknowledgements

'Triptych' from *Peace Talks* by Andrew Motion (Faber and Faber 2015) reprinted by permission of the author.

Every effort has been made to seek permission to use copyright material reproduced in this book. The author apologises for those cases where permission might not have been sought and, if notified, will formally seek permission at the earliest opportunity.

Acknowledgements

I would like to thank Nicholas Hardyman who helped organise and produce the original readings on Good Fridays in the University Church, Oxford. My very great thanks to Penny Boxall, Education Officer at the University Church and herself a poet, who gave me a great deal of valuable editorial advice.

CHRISTIAN
ALTERNATIVE

Christian Alternative

THE NEW OPEN SPACES

Throughout the two thousand years of Christian tradition there have been, and still are, groups and individuals that exist in the margins and upon the edge of faith. But in Christianity's contrapuntal history it has often been these outcasts and pioneers that have forged contemporary orthodoxy out of former radicalism as belief evolves to engage with and encompass the ever-changing social and scientific realities. Real faith lies not in the comfortable certainties of the Orthodox, but somewhere in a half-glimpsed hinterland on the dirt track to Emmaus, where the Death of God meets the Resurrection, where the supernatural Christ meets the historical Jesus, and where the revolution liberates both the oppressed and the oppressors.

Welcome to Christian Alternative... a space at the edge where the light shines through.
If you have enjoyed this book, why not tell other readers by posting a review on your preferred book site.

Recent bestsellers from Christian Alternative are:

Bread Not Stones
The Autobiography of An Eventful Life
Una Kroll
The spiritual autobiography of a truly remarkable woman
and a history of the struggle for ordination in the Church of
England.
Paperback: 978-1-78279-804-0 ebook: 978-1-78279-805-7

The Quaker Way
A Rediscovery
Rex Ambler
Although fairly well known, Quakerism is not well understood.
The purpose of this book is to explain how Quakerism works as
a spiritual practice.
Paperback: 978-1-78099-657-8 ebook: 978-1-78099-658-5

Blue Sky God
The Evolution of Science and Christianity
Don MacGregor
Quantum consciousness, morphic fields and blue-sky
thinking about God and Jesus the Christ.
Paperback: 978-1-84694-937-1 ebook: 978-1-84694-938-8

Celtic Wheel of the Year
Tess Ward
An original and inspiring selection of prayers combining
Christian and Celtic Pagan traditions, and interweaving their
calendars into a single pattern of prayer for every morning
and night of the year.
Paperback: 978-1-90504-795-6

The Gay Gospels
Good News for Lesbian, Gay, Bisexual, and Transgendered People
Keith Sharpe
This book refutes the idea that the Bible is homophobic
and makes visible the gay lives and validated homoerotic
experience to be found in it.
Paperback: 978-1-84694-548-9 ebook: 978-1-78099-063-7

The Illusion of "Truth"
The Real Jesus Behind the Grand Myth
Thomas Nehrer
Nehrer, uniquely aware of Reality's integrated flow, elucidates
Jesus' penetrating, often mystifying insights – exposing
widespread religious, scholarly and skeptical fallacy.
Paperback: 978-1-78279-548-3 ebook: 978-1-78279-551-3

Fingerprints of Fire, Footprints of Peace
A Spiritual Manifesto from a Jesus Perspective
Noel Moules
Christian spirituality with attitude. Fourteen provocative
pictures, from Radical Mystic to Messianic Anarchist, that
explore identity, destiny, values and activism.
Paperback: 978-1-84694-612-7 ebook: 978-1-78099-903-6

Readers of ebooks can buy or view any of these bestsellers by clicking on the live link in the title. Most titles are published in paperback and as an ebook. Paperbacks are available in traditional bookshops. Both print and ebook formats are available online.

Find more titles and sign up to our readers' newsletter at
http://www.johnhuntpublishing.com/christianity
Follow us on Facebook at
https://www.facebook.com/ChristianAlternative